A SHORT HISTORY
OF
ENGLISH DRAMA
BY
B. IFOR EVANS

GREENWOOD PRESS, PUBLISHERS
WESTPORT, CONNECTICUT

Library of Congress Cataloging in Publication Data

Evans, Benjamin Ifor, Baron Evans of Hungershall, 1899-
   A short history of English drama.

   Reprint of the 1950 ed. published by Penguin Books,
Harmondsworth, Eng.
   1. English drama--History and criticism.
I. Title.
[PR625.E8 1978]   822'.009   77-27446
ISBN 0-8371-9072-X

First published 1948

Reprinted with the permission of Granada Publishing Limited

Reprinted in 1978 by Greenwood Press, Inc.,
51 Riverside Avenue
Westport, CT. 06880

Printed in the United States of America

10 9 8 7 6 5 4 3 2 1

TO
Sir Barry Jackson
WHO HAS DEVOTED HIMSELF
SO UNSELFISHLY TO THE DRAMA
IN ENGLAND

CONTENTS

I

Introductory

THE history of the drama in England is more than an account of authors and plays, for it concerns the whole continuing tradition of the theatre. To the creation of a play the author is only one contributor. For success co-partnership is essential, and in it actors, producer, designers and technicians must also be constituents. Conditions leading to the happy union of all these elements have occurred only infrequently in the history of the English theatre. When they have prevailed, as in Elizabethan times, the gain has been immediately apparent. Many of the Elizabethan dramatists and managers who were in control of production were also actors. Whatever may be unknown about Shakespeare's life it can at least be affirmed with certainty that he was an actor, interested in theatrical enterprises, so that during his years in London he spent a considerable portion of his time in the theatre.

The excessive and inevitable attachment of criticism to the author has had a number of unhappy consequences. In the first place an illusion, utterly false, has been created that drama can be appreciated in independence of the theatre. Unfortunately two of the noblest names in English literature have helped to perpetuate this heresy: Milton in *Samson Agonistes* and Thomas Hardy in *The Dynasts*. Milton's early interest in the drama was modified by his growing antagonism and natural hatred of the type of comedy popular in the Restoration theatre. Thomas Hardy, whose experience of the attempts to adapt his novels for the stage had been unfortunate, went as far in his preface to *The Dynasts* as to speculate 'whether mental performance alone may not eventually be the fate of all drama other than that of contemporary or frivolous life'. The same detachment of the author from the living world of the theatre has been responsible for the fact that our literature is strewn with wholly un-actable plays by names as great as those of S. T. Coleridge, Wordsworth and Swinburne.

The damaging results of such a condition can be seen at their worst in the history of Shakespearian study in England. Every year tens of thousands of children in state-endowed schools are made to attend to Shakespeare's text by teachers the great majority of whom cannot speak verse, have no interest in the drama, and seldom, if ever, see a play on the stage. The anomaly continues when scholars write learnedly on all aspects of Shakespeare's text and age, but never interest themselves in the production of his work. There are of course notable exceptions, but it is sobering to recall that as I write Shakespeare is being more frequently performed in the Soviet Union than in England.

The actor himself has not been without his share of responsibility in this detachment of the stage from society. His art makes him inevitably a man apart. He goes to work when other men go to dine, and his hours of labour are inevitably other men's periods of leisure. In Elizabethan times the law set him apart from his fellowmen, and in some ways he has insisted on some form of isolation even to the present day. He has maintained, all too

often, that his art is some secret which the layman cannot understand.

At certain periods he has shown himself devoid of
general culture, and as a consequence has failed to make
adequate contact with whatever was best and most distinguished in the society of his time. His art has often
seemed to affect his personality, as if the task of filling
one role after another, and so exposing himself to the
public, had left his own character rather nebulous, in
some instances almost a vacuum. Further, a certain
pathos surrounds the actor, for his art can live only as
long as his own person is there to reveal it.

The path of the dramatic author in England has usually
not been an easy one. As distinct from the author who
writes books for sale to the public he has had to face the
incredible vagaries of the law of Censorship. In Tudor
times plays were censored as part of the general law by
which all activities within the State were controlled. The
authority came from the Sovereign in Council and was
delegated normally to the Master of Revels. So conditions
continued until Cromwell ordered the closing of all public
theatres from 1642. Though drama survived until the
Restoration of 1660 by an underground movement of
private performances, Cromwell's action fastened on the
theatre the stigma of puritan disapproval to which it had
already been subjected in Elizabethan times, and this has
remained in some modified form until the present day.
With the Restoration the theatre discovered in Charles II
a monarch who appreciated the arts, and though plays
were nominally censored by the Lord Chamberlain's
Master of the Revels, the drama enjoyed great freedom
from 1660 to 1685. With the Revolution of 1688 condi-

tions became more severe. In 1698 Jeremy Collier published his *Short View of the Immorality and Profaneness of the English Stage,* which attacked the licence and obscenity of the Restoration dramatists, of Wycherley, Dryden and Congreve. William III, in 1697, duly passed an order condemning the licentiousness of plays and ordered that in future the players should not 'presume to act anything in any play contrary to religion and good manners, as they shall answer at their utmost peril'.* The theatre was already being treated differently from other types of literary production, but it was not yet manacled. The story of how that happened is one of the most extraordinary in English literary history.

In 1728 John Gay's *The Beggar's Opera* was performed at Lincoln s Inn Fields with great success, and London audiences saw in Macheath an attack on Sir Robert Walpole's system of government by bribery. Gay followed his triumph with *Polly,* which the authorities prohibited though this did not prevent the successful publication of the play. Henry Fielding in 1736 composed an open satire on corruption entitled *The Historical Register.* Walpole replied with his Act on the Censorship of plays (10 Geo. II, c. 19). Not that he openly condemned the plays which he attacked. More cautiously and subtly he found conveniently at hand an obscene play, *The Golden Rump,* to prevent whose performance the whole of the English drama had to be enslaved. Walpole's Act of 1737 placed the licensing of plays under the Lord Chamberlain, and so the law remained until the Theatres Act of 1843. Even this did not change the position in any material way. For the Lord Chamberlain

* *The Censor and the Theatres* by John Palmer (Fisher Unwin), 1912.

could prohibit performance whenever in his opinion 'it was necessary for the preservation of good manners and decorum, or of the public peace'. The Lord Chamberlain could license theatres and plays, and in special circumstances he could summarily close theatres. The medieval writers of miracle and morality plays, most of the Elizabethan and Restoration dramatists would not have had their work produced if they had been forced to submit it to the censorship of the Lord Chamberlain as it existed after 1737. Politics, religion, and history were all affected as themes for presentation, as indeed were most of the subjects dealing with the profounder aspects of human life. Thomas Hardy summarised the view of many writers when he made a statement in 1909 to the 'Joint Committee on Stage Plays (Censorship)': 'All I can say is that something or other appears to deter men of letters, who have other channels for communicating with the public, from writing for the stage'.

The adequate performance of plays necessitates proper buildings, and here the position in England has been distressingly inadequate for the last three centuries. The Elizabethan theatre, though not an elaborate structure, was skilfully designed for its purpose. The development of the modern theatre dates from the period of the Restoration of 1660. From that time onwards the attention given to scenic architecture in England has lagged behind developments in France, Germany and Russia. All experiment was seriously affected by the fact that from the Restoration to the Theatres Act of 1843 the legitimate drama was largely confined to a few 'Patent' theatres.* In the early eighteenth century these were Drury Lane and a small theatre in Lincoln's Inn Fields, opened in

* See *The Development of the Theatre* by Allardyce Nicoll (1927).

1714. After 1732 Covent Garden was substituted as the second patent theatre.

The Licensing Act of 1737 ordained the closing of all theatres except Drury Lane and Covent Garden. In point of fact other theatres maintained their existence and a special licence for periodical performances was granted to the Theatre Royal in the Haymarket. The patent theatres, to retain their position, increased in size whenever they had to be rebuilt, until Drury Lane rebuilt in 1812 could seat 3200 and Covent Garden as rebuilt in 1809 could seat 3000. The Act of 1843 destroyed the monopoly of the patent theatres, and many of the present London theatres were constructed between 1843 and the end of the sixties. Unfortunately it was a period in which there was little that was exhilarating either in the tradition of architecture or in the theatre itself. Almost one feels that the puritan tradition must in some cryptic way have revenged itself on audiences through the architecture of the theatre. Drama in England has had to endure a struggle against prejudice among large sections of the public, and from the State discouragement of a particularly unintelligent order. The degree to which initiative can survive against such difficulties can be seen in a number of instances such as the history of the triumph of Lilian Baylis at the 'Old Vic' and Sadler's Wells. This introduction is written in 1946 when for the first time the State by its Charter to the Arts Council of Great Britain gives official and financial support to the Arts, including the Art of Drama. Much remains to be done, first in the removal of prohibitions from the dramatist, and secondly in the provision of worthy buildings, not only in London, but throughout the country.

2

The Origins – Miracles – Moralities – Interludes

THE history of the drama can be made to look too simple, as if it were a regular succession from miracle play to morality, from morality play to interlude, and from interlude to a regular comedy and tragedy, and so on until modern times. The historian is in danger of treating literary forms as if they were organic growths. In point of fact there are many overlappings, and different types of entertainment, the new and the old, flourish at the same time. Men had not forgotten the miracle plays when Shakespeare was writing, and while listening to the astounding power of his new language they still retained the power of enjoying those simpler dramatic forms. Further, the records from which the history of the drama can be constructed are very incomplete. Very few plays, for instance, are extant in the period immediately preceding Marlowe and his contemporaries. The history of acting, of the stage, of costumes and décor, is even more inadequate. The historian who tries to tell a complete story is relying to a considerable extent on theory and speculation.

It is usual to begin with medieval drama. In the early Christian period there had been a reaction among the Christians against Roman plays, and this for two reasons. The Christians objected on principle to acting, basing themselves on certain biblical texts, such as Deuteronomy xxii. 5: 'The woman shall not wear that which pertaineth unto a man, neither shall a man put on a woman's garment: for all that do so are abomination unto the Lord thy God'. That argument was sufficiently alive when Milton wrote his *Areopagitica* for him to oppose it with texts from St. Paul.

More forcible was the rational and practical Christian objection to the excesses of the late Roman stage. At that period the stage had little room for literary drama. The theatre, which at times was vast enough to hold 20,000 people, was a place of spectacle, and the actor often a slave or freedman. The productions, when they were not spectacles, were farce of a gross character. It is true that in Seneca the Elizabethans remembered one dramatist who wrote in the days of Nero, but his plays were composed not to be performed but for contemplation in the study. By the sixth century the incursions of the barbarians and the growing strength of the Christians had undermined the stage, and with few exceptions it ceased to exist as it had been known in Roman days.

In the Dark Ages, from the sixth to the tenth century, the theatre largely disappears as far as any record in documents is concerned, though probably it remained in a submerged way. If the stage disappears, the actor survives, and survives without a stage and without a drama. The poetry of Chaucer and Langland has frequent references to travelling players, 'Jonglers' and 'Joculators', and Langland condemned them as a social pest. These travelling players were of a number of different types. The German tribes before their settlement in Britain, and for some time afterwards, had their professional tale tellers or *Scops*. A mention of them is made in *Beowulf*, and that poem is told as a *Scop's* tale. One of the most beautiful of Old English poems is *Widsith* ('The Far

Traveller'), which tells of the life of a *Scop*. The Christian attitude to the *Scop* was one of opposition for he was a part of a pagan civilisation. Sometimes a Christian bias seems to have been given to his function and his tales modified and given a Christian emphasis.

A less dignified performer was the 'Mime'. He probably came into Britain through a Latin influence and with him were tumblers, dancers, and jokers of varying degrees of disrepute. The activities of such players were sufficient to cause the Church by the thirteenth century to pass a number of decrees restricting their activities. From the twelfth century to the fourteenth the 'minstrels' occupied an important part in the social life. Some of them were resident at Court and in the great houses, and some were strollers. They made songs for war and they praised and abused personalities. Even the Church which formerly condemned such performers came to recognise them and sometimes made use of them. It is difficult to know whether their activities ever approached a theatrical production. Apart from these individual players there grew up in the villages a number of activities of a folk nature. They had sufficient prominence for attacks to be made on them by the thirteenth century. Such celebrations were usually seasonal and of a communal nature. They were a method of indulging a natural desire for miming and were an expression of a normal urge to commemorate the spring or harvest time or the autumn.

Not all the seasonal activities were confined to the villages. A similar desire for dramatic expression showed itself among the lower orders of the clergy, particularly in masking and dancing and in the burlesque of the offices of the Church. Sir E. K. Chambers, the great historian of this period, sums up the psychology behind these burlesques by saying that 'It was largely an ebullition of the natural lout beneath the cassock'.* One of the most popular of these mock ceremonies was that of the Boy Bishop, in which the choir boys took on themselves the main functions performed normally by the clerical dignitaries.

All these and similar activities showed the survival of a play instinct though they were removed from drama even of a rudimentary type.   Yet in the Middle Ages out of these conditions and activities drama re-established itself. It is a complex story of which the most important fact remains that while at the beginning of the Dark Ages the Church attempted to suppress the drama, at the beginning of the Middle Ages something very much like the drama was instituted in the Church itself.

The Mass, which had early developed as the central element in the service of the Church, had a certain dramatic element within it, particularly when on certain days special features were added which increased the dramatic significance. Out of this there came the presentation by voices chanting in Latin certain crucial scenes in the Christian story, such as those of the Birth and Resurrection of Christ. For instance, two groups of voices would sing, the first asking

Whom do you seek in the sepulchre, you followers of Christ?

and the second group would reply

Jesus of Nazareth, who was crucified, O you who are of heaven.

* *The Medieval Stage*, 2 vols. (Oxford University Press), 1903.

Such presentations may have begun simply, but they became elaborate, and attached to the words was a ritual and a dumb show. It is easy to imagine that these liturgical plays were more realistic than they probably were, but some step towards a dramatic presentation had obviously taken place, particularly at the festivals of Christmas, and of the celebration of the Resurrection.

Once established, they had an important effect on the history of the drama. They were in all likelihood fully established by the middle of the fourteenth century and by the middle of the fifteenth they had become secular-ised. Again it is difficult not to make the process seem simpler than it probably was. The liturgical plays at Christmas and the Resurrection were extended to in-clude other incidents, until a fairly complete cycle of the biblical story had been made. For instance, the story of the Creation was easily presented in this manner, and with each addition the liturgical play grew closer to legitimate drama. The element of devotion decreased as the element of dramatic presentation increased.

With these extensions in the plays there came changes in the place of presentation. Again it is difficult to say exactly when these occurred. Nor is it necessary to assume that they were simultaneous in all places. In general it would seem that the plays began in the choir, and from the choir went to the nave, and from the nave to the out-side of the church. When the crowds outside the church became too unseemly for the holy precincts the play moved to the market-place, or joined a succession of plays which were shifted from one position to another in procession around the city. The change illustrates the desire of the clerical authorities to be less intimately associated with the drama, and it is obvious that once the play was in the market-place, and in competition with other forms of entertainment, its character would increase in secularity.

The civic corporations organised the plays, and exercised some censorship over the choice and the method of presentation, while the craft guilds produced them and bore the cost. Each member of a craft guild paid a contribution towards the cost of production. We have to wait until 1946 before anything of this kind was to happen again after the sixteenth century, when the Amalgamated Engineers' Union began a season of plays entitled 'Theatre '46'. While in the fourteenth century the craft guilds wrote plays about God and the Christian story, in 1946 the Amalgamated Engineers' Union wrote a play about the Amalgamated Engineers' Union. Of the many cycles that once existed a few have survived, most notably those of Chester, York, 'Towneley' (or Wakefield) and Coventry.

Of these, the cycle of plays produced at York is interesting because it is complete, and it is known to have been performed as late as 1580 and as early as the early fourteenth century. The plays have not the outstanding features of the 'Towneley' cycle, but their verse, which is written in a combination of stanza and alliteration, is vivid and competent. Many of the plays in the York cycle are an elaboration of the biblical narratives without obvious dramatic features, but the anonymous writers are able to deal well with scenes of pathos such as Abraham's sacrifice of Isaac. The sincerity and tender simplicity of sentiment are again shown in the play of the flight into Egypt. The Wakefield or 'Towneley' cycle has some plays in common with those of York, but, in addition, it has five plays of a striking originality. These are the plays of Noah with his children, the First Shepherds' Play, the Second Shepherds' Play, the Play of King Herod, and the Play of Christ before Cayphus. In these plays there is close vivid description of a realistic nature. Such can be found in the description of the ship in the Noah play. Further, there is dialogue of a most natural, human and contemporary kind. It can be seen in the vivid characterisation of Noah's wife as a shrew. At the same time the dramatist can deal solemnly with such passages as God's discussion with Noah, and throughout he can manipulate a difficult stanza.

The outstanding success of this dramatist is the Second Shepherds' Play. This stands apart in achievement from all other English miracle plays. It opens with a realistic account of the woes of shepherds and with a virulent attack on women. There is no attempt in this early movement to remember the sacred aspect of the theme, which is after all the celebration of the Virgin Mother. After a song by the shepherds, Mak the sheep-stealer enters and complains of the noise that the children make. He says that his wife bears too many children. After a time the shepherds sleep and Mak steals a sheep. The scene shifts to Mak's home where his wife is made to pretend that the sheep is a child in a bed. Mak returns to the shepherds and after waking them says that his wife has given birth to a boy. The shepherds wish to give this child a present and when they arrive in Mak's home, after a comic interlude, they discover the stolen sheep. Then they hear the angel and in song they try to imitate him, and so they come to Bethlehem to honour the Infant Christ. It is difficult to know precisely what went through the mind of either the dramatist or the audience, for the whole of the early comic part of the play seems to repeat in grotesque form the incidents which the religious element in the play is celebrating.

Apart from the miracle plays, and developing after they were established, were a series of Morality plays, in which the characters represent abstract qualities. At first sight this seems rather a dull method for drama, but the abstract qualities are given very lively human features. One of the earliest of these Moralities is the *Castle of Perseverance* (of the early fifteenth century) and the play is so finished that it suggests that there must have been others in the same tradition not now extant. The dialogue is written in an elaborate rhyming stanza, and the play gives an account of man's life from birth to his appearance at the Seat of Judgment. The most famous of the English Moralities is the play of *Everyman* which, it has been established, is the same as the Dutch play *Elckerlijk*. The English play was made about 1500 and its popularity is shown by the frequency with which it was reprinted in the sixteenth century. Though its theme is not unlike that of the *Castle of Perseverance* it is much less prolix, with a fine quality of directness and pathos in its verse. Its theme is given the same human quality as is found in *Pilgrim's Progress*, which is a very similar story. The audience knows that both these works are allegories and yet they affect the mind in the same way as a piece of human adventure. Though the characters in *Everyman* are abstract figures, they have more variety than the individual persons derived from biblical narrative. They are far more contemporary than the biblical figures, and

the morality method gives more opportunity for independent treatment by the dramatist.

Everyman is a man of his time, close to the audience,
and in this strange way the morality play gains a realism
of its own. The strength of *Everyman* lies also in the skill
with which the scenes are developed. There is not the
stale obviousness which marks some of the other morality
plays. The story, although it is an allegorical one, seems
to be the story of an ordinary journey. God sends Death
to Everyman and tells him to prepare for a journey, and
there is a simple poignancy in the language of Death's
first talk with Everyman. After Death's visit Everyman
appeals to his friends, to Fellowship, Kinsmen, and
Goods, but they all desert him. Good Deeds alone will
go with him, and there is again a definite dramatic quality
in the lines recording Everyman's encounter with Good
Deeds. So at each stage of Everyman's journey the
abstract is made concrete by lively figures and human
situations.

Some of the moralities had comic elements. The play of
Mankynd of the late fifteenth century is one of the best
known of this type. Its whole tone differs from that of
Everyman. Mankynd is attacked by three rascals, Nowte,
Newgyse and Nowadays, and he is befriended by Mercy.
The three villains are real and contemporary figures.
They have comedy and coarseness, and though the play
may have little construction, it has a vivid quality in its
language. The morality play was used in many ways, as is
shown in John Skelton's *Magnyfycence*, where the theme
is political and not didactic or religious. Skelton shows
how Fancy, armed with a false letter of introduction,
comes to Magnificence who later is led to destruction,

though finally rescued by the teaching of the virtues. The figure of Magnificence is Skelton's satire against Wolsey.

Apart from the elements of secularism which appear in the miracle and morality plays there develops an 'Interlude', which is frequently made and produced solely for its dramatic value. One of the earliest is *Hyckescorner* of the beginning of the sixteenth century. The title is the name of one of the characters. The play has little dramatic strength, and follows the lines of a morality play, though its theme is humanistic rather than didactic. The main plot is the conversion of Freewill and Imagination through the agency of Pity, Perseverance, and Contemplation. The household of Sir Thomas More had a taste for such dramatic entertainments and around More there were those who could make interludes and who had the means of circulating them. John Rastell, a printer and a writer of interludes, married Sir Thomas More's sister. John Heywood, the writer of interludes, is Rastell's son-in-law. William Rastell, who was John Rastell's son, was the printer of Heywood's plays. In such a community where drama and wit were both understood the Interlude had an opportunity of development.

One of the plays whose authorship has been claimed for John Rastell is that of *Calisto and Melebea*. The writer based his play on an English version of the Spanish rogue story of *Celestina*. The Spanish tale tells of the love inevitable and romantic of Calisto for Melebea, and the outstanding character is Celestina, a bawd who is portrayed as firmly as Pandarus, and who brings the two lovers together. The intrigues multiply and lead to a tragic conclusion. The English writer fails to employ the Spanish story to the full and while he opens with the two lovers he has such a firm eye on his 'moral conclusion' that he achieves little by way of plot. *The Four Elements* and *Gentleness and Nobility* are other interludes which have been assigned to John Rastell's authorship. *The Four Elements* is in the form of a dialogue, or discussion. Its purpose is to instruct 'Humanity' in the nature of the four elements (earth, water, air, and fire). 'Humanity' receives the information from 'Nature' whose points are further explained by 'Studious Desire', who calls in the help of 'Experience', while 'Sensual Appetite' disturbs the instruction of 'Studious Desire'.

John Heywood, whose plays were written soon after 1520, is the most considerable figure in the history of the Interlude. Married to Rastell's daughter, he was in the centre of More's circle and it has been surmised that some of his plays were revised by More himself. Most of them are arguments and disputations between a number of characters with the addition of a comic element. Of these the neatest in its movement is *The Play of the Wether*. Jupiter appoints Merry Report to summon the people before him so that he may listen to the complaints of mortals on the weather. Merry Report ('a vyce'), is a comic rascal who addresses his master in the witty and impertinent conversation which Shakespeare's fools employ. Jupiter discovers that all the suitors require different types of weather so he decides to continue giving them an assortment, and the play ends with a sort of 'Magnificat' by all the suppliants.

Another of Heywood's plays was *The Four P.P.* which is described as a 'new and very merry interlude of a palmer, a pardoner, a pothycary and a pedlar'. It is a discussion, and like *The Play of the Wether* it has a monotonous movement. Its strength, as in all of Heywood's pieces, lies in the vigour of the dialogue. The discussion centres on the topic of which of the four men can tell the biggest lie. The climax comes in the story of the pardoner, who tells of a visit to Hell, and of the rescue of a shrew. The palmer breaks in with the question 'Are there shrews in Hell?' He is surprised, for in all his travels he has never met a woman out of patience. His lie wins. Lest too much weight be attached to all this, the play has a tail-piece:

> To pass the time in this without offence
> Was the cause why the maker did make it
> And so we humbly beseech you take it!

The purpose of the play is comedy and not didacticism.

There remain two Interludes by Heywood which have a more ample dramatic interest: these are *Johan Johan the Husband, Tyb his Wife and Sir John the Priest* and *A Merry Play Between the Pardoner and the Friar, the Curate and Neighbour Pratte*. The first of these is lively though crude. The plot turns on the love-making of Tyb and the priest, and the timid uneasiness of the husband. Whatever its limitations, the play has moved from mere discussion to dramatic action. The *Merry Play* is of a pardoner and a friar who come to the same church and try to preach at the same time. This leads to a fight with the parish priest and neighbour Pratte. Comedy has arrived at something of a separate existence in Heywood, though as yet there are few indications of its employment in anything but the crudest forms. Another memorable Interlude which showed dramatic development within the form was *Thersytes* (of about 1530) a play probably designed for children. The theme, which is derived, is a comic study of cowardice and follows in some simple ways the mood which Ibsen was later to exploit so magnificently in *Peer Gynt*.

If one had to judge the Interlude solely by these plays one would be unable to place its dramatic achievement very high. Fortunately there was discovered within living memory the play of *Fulgens and Lucrece* by Henry Medwall, Chaplin to Cardinal Morton. Of a date as early as 1497, this play shows by the cunning of its form and the adroitness of its dialogue how far the secular dramatist had progressed. The plot is based on a renaissance Latin discourse by Bonaccorso entitled *De Vera Nobilitate*. A Roman Senator has a daughter Lucres, who has two suitors, one of humble birth and the other a noble. She asks her father what to do and her father asks the Senate. The two suitors plead before the Senate and nothing is decided. This unpromising plot is handled in the play with great skill. Medwall introduces the play with the dialogue of two spectators, who are present to see the entertainment at a banquet, and their talk suggests that there were already present in England companies of players so well dressed that the gallants emulated their fashions. The two spectators prepare the audience for the argument. The plot is then developed dramatically for the suitors plead not to the Senate but in turn to the lady, who herself decides for the poor and virtuous suitor. There is a comic sub-plot, and the two spectators take sides, and finally enter the main theme as farcical suitors for Lucres's maid. This play is an indication of what could be done already in the fifteenth century, independently of Italian models. Further, it is a warning how incomplete are the records on which the history of drama is based, for this play was unknown until a copy of it appeared in the Mostyn sale in 1919.

On the evidence which exists it is impossible to trace a regular development from the Interludes to the more elaborate drama which follows. New influences came in, the plays of Plautus and Terence, the comedy of Italy, and in tragedy the influence of Seneca. All this disturbed any regular native development from the Interlude to Elizabethan drama. The new forms were far more ambitious than the old, but they did not entirely replace them. As has been already recorded the York Miracle plays were performed late in the sixteenth century, while some of the cycles continue to the seventeenth century. It is to the newer interests that the great dramatists largely attach themselves, though the more their work is studied the more the ghosts of the older drama can be seen in the themes and values of their work. The break in comedy is much less definite than in tragedy, for the native tradition in comedy had been strong and vital. In tragedy there had been no native models.

3

The Beginnings of Tragedy,
of the History Play, and of Comedy –
The Development of the Theatre

THE specimens of plays extant from the sixteenth century are very incomplete. The conclusion which results from reading them is that drama made a sudden and spectacular step forward somewhere between 1530 and 1580. For 1530 is the probable date of *Calisto and Melebea* and *The Play of the Wether*, while by 1588 audiences were already familiar with *Tamburlaine*. Some influence had incited dramatists to far· more ambitious achievements, and fortunately their genius was adequate to answer their needs.

In tragedy, the outstanding new influence was that of Seneca. He was known to the men of the renaissance period as the author of ten tragedies. Seneca, a Latin writer of the ˙ime of Nero, and the author of 'closet' dramas, had studied Greek drama, particularly the tragedies of Euripides. He retained the chorus of Greek drama, though he placed it at the end of his acts, and did not allow it to interfere in the play. He retained something of the pattern of Greek drama, though its spirit did not remain. Greek drama was religious in origin and the speeches were governed and disciplined by that consideration. In Seneca that religious element had passed, and the long, declamatory speeches remained shorn of their original purpose. He retained the 'messenger' who was employed in Greek drama to reveal action that had taken place 'off' stage, but he gave his long speeches usually a narrative rather than a dramatic quality. Mingled with the long speeches, and in violent contrast with them, were passages of *stichomythia* (dialogue in alternate lines of verse employed in argument). The themes Seneca employed were nominally the themes of Greek drama. But for the awe and terror which they possess he substituted an element of mere horror. In Greek drama the sense of Fate or Will behind the individuals present in the action elevated the conception of the tragedy. For this Seneca substituted personal revenge as the main motive for action, and following his example this was employed in Elizabethan drama. Delighting in horrors Seneca introduced the Ghost almost as a definite member of the 'dramatis personae'. In language he was rhetorical and bombastic and his delight in horrors was paralleled by his equal affection for moral discourses in the manner of Polonius.

It seems strange at first sight that this unacted dramatist of the time of Nero should become the major influence on English tragedy in the sixteenth century. But he was, in the first place, far more easily accessible than any Greek dramatist, for few of the Elizabethan dramatists could have read a play in Greek. To the medieval elements in the sixteenth-century mind there was an obvious appeal in his long moral discourses, while to the renaissance mind there was the advantage that Seneca seemed to give all the form of Greek drama, the unities, the chorus, and the values behind the themes. Above all, Seneca's indulgence in horror delighted men who knew a world where death was familiar and violence a part of the scene both domestic and political. Thus the main classical influence on English tragedy is Latin and not Greek.

In Italy among the renaissance writers most influenced by the Greeks were Trissino and his followers, but in the forties of the sixteenth century a more popular dramatist on the Senecan model ousts Trissino and replaces him in popular favour. In England something similar happens. At first a number of writers seem attracted to Greek drama, and then there emerge the popular, Senecan writers who capture the stage. The influence in England appears mainly after 1560. Before that date classical names appear in a few of the Interludes, of which *Thersytes* is the main example and one of Seneca's plays *Troades* is performed in Latin, at Cambridge. In the sixties the influence is considerable. Seneca's plays are translated, and in 1561–62 *Gorboduc* by Thomas Norton and Thomas Sackville, the first English Senecan tragedy, was acted before the Queen at Whitehall. Some learned Senecan plays were performed at the Inns of Court and a group of Interludes (*Appius and Virginia*, 1567; *Damon and Pythias*, 1564; *Horestes*, 1566–7; *Cambyses*, 1569), made a link between the academic and the popular tradition. The period 1570–80 is difficult to define because the records are so scanty, but from 1580 onwards there is evidence of an increased Senecan influence. By 1581 all the 'ten tragedies' had been translated, and Thomas Newton issued his collection of *Seneca His Ten Tragedies Translated into English*. There was a revival of influence by the performance of some of his plays at the Universities, while learned imitations were also produced, *Ricardus Tertius* at Cambridge, and *The Misfortunes of Arthur* at the Inns of Court. By the end of the decade competent dramatists had captured a popular Senecan tradition for the ordinary stage. The outstanding example was Thomas Kyd's *The Spanish Tragedy* (1587-9). Senecan influence was present in Marlowe and Shakespeare and was revived later by Ben Jonson in *Sejanus* and in *Catiline*.

Meanwhile the English Chronicle play had shown a parallel development with Senecan tragedy, though largely independent of it. Senecan tragedy was European while the Chronicle play was English. Some of the elements which went to its making were the medieval pageants and the plays of the Lives of Saints, such as are known to have existed on the Life of St. George. Further, there is evidence that there were some local traditions for the dramatic rendering of historical events.

The Chronicle play was one which relied for its sources on the English chronicles and dealt with some period of English history. It gained in the hands of Shakespeare an identity with tragedy, for to contemporary audiences *Lear* and *Macbeth* were chronicle plays. John Bale's *Kyng Johan* (1536), though the title promises a historical play, is a morality full of Protestant propaganda. Bale began life as a Catholic but was converted to Protestantism. After his conversion he wrote a play in defence of King John whom he presents as a Protestant hero. *Gorboduc*, 1562, is important in that it links the Senecan tradition of tragedy with the native chronicle play: it takes an English story from Geoffrey of Monmouth and develops it on the Senecan pattern. Thomas Legge in *Ricardus Tertius* (1579) attempted to use the learned Latin Senecan tradition for an English theme. Richard III's career, as Shakespeare was later to discover, developed very easily from history into the pattern of tragedy. *The Misfortunes of Arthur* (1588), to which reference has already been made, was another attempt to apply Senecan form to national themes. *Locrine*, sometimes ascribed to Kyd, was an attempt to introduce more popular elements while keeping to the Senecan pattern.

The Chronicle play answered one element of the demand for a popular presentation of history. That the demand was real and persistent can be seen in the popularity of such a collection of historical poems as *The Mirror for Magistrates*, or later in the success of the chronicle poems of Daniel and Drayton. It can be seen also in the continued popularity of the chroniclers themselves, of Grafton and John Stow, and of Ralph Holinshed on whose work Shakespeare relied in such an impressive way.

The earliest of the extant chronicles is *The Famous Victories of Henry V* (1588): it is a formless piece but it had considerable popularity. No attempt is made here at tragedy, but history is dramatically presented by a number of incidents taken from the reigns of Henry IV and Henry V. Shakespeare, who knew this early piece, went over the same ground with a more ample inclusion of historical material in *I* and *II Henry IV* and in *Henry V*. The Prince and his low companions are already present in the early play, but there is no Falstaff. The Senecan model is not employed, but unfortunately no other model has replaced it. From the shapelessness of a piece such as this one realises what the dramatists gained by the example of Seneca, whatever may have been the incidental liabilities of his influence. *The Troublesome Raigne of King John* (1588–90), which has Holinshed's

B–ED

chronicle as a source, was an advance on the formlessness of *The Famous Victories*. The presentation of material is still diffuse, and even Shakespeare, who knew this play, failed to give the same theme a full unity. The comic matter is not so clownish as in *The Famous Victories*, and the chronicle matter is handled with an eye to dramatic propriety. The spirit is Protestant, which Shakespeare converts to a national atmosphere.

The years around the Armada mark the great period of the popularity of the chronicle and history play. Peele's *Edward I* (printed 1593), apparently a hastily written piece, seems to mark no advance on the general type. *The True Chronicle of King Leir* (1594, printed 1605) has a rough effectiveness and holds a proud place as the predecessor of Shakespeare's most profound tragedy. Similarly *The True Tragedie of Richard III* (printed 1594) is a source for the development of the chronicle into tragedy in Shakespeare's *Richard III*. With Marlowe's *Edward II* (printed 1594) a writer of genius has disciplined the chronicle into tragedy, and the events of twenty years are reduced to what may be digested in a play. Nor is the tragedy diffuse, for it concentrates on an uncommon conception of a weak man as a central protagonist, a type found again, with ample modifications, in Shakespeare's *Richard II*. It must be confessed however that perhaps *Edward II* is a better play to talk about than to see on the stage. Probably one of Shakespeare's earliest tasks in the theatre was his share in the three parts of *Henry VI*, and how great that share was remains a disputed problem in Shakespearian criticism. It was from his attachment to the Chronicle play that he discovered such original forms as *Henry IV* and *Henry V*, and it was through this same type that he discovered his major way into tragedy.

While there were these developments in tragedy and Chronicle play during the sixteenth century there were also changes in comedy. As has already been suggested, comedy had a strong native tradition and might well have developed successfully, though in a different way, without foreign influence. The study of two Latin authors, of Plautus and Terence, gave to English comedy a sense of pattern which it had not previously possessed. This Latin influence was partly due to a number of schoolmasters who read Latin plays with their pupils. The first comedy on classical models is *Ralph Roister Doister* (1553–4, printed 1566), and this is the work of a schoolmaster, Nicholas Udall, who was a master first at Eton, and later at Westminster. The main plot of the play is simple enough: Ralph Roister Doister is in love with Dame Christian Custance. He fails in his love owing to his own pride and stupidity. To further his suit he employs a comic rascal Matthew Merygreeke who is developed into one of the major characters in the play. A more effective comedy was *Gammer Gurton's Needle* (about 1553, printed 1575) which is described as 'a right pithy, pleasant and merry comedy'. The authorship is ascribed to 'Mr. S. Master of Art'. Whoever the author was he had learned something from Latin drama, but in character, scene and plot he is native and original. His plot is farcical. Gammer Gurton was mending the breeches of her man Hodge. They were 'foul betorn', and needed a patch as 'broad as thy cap'. As she was mending them she spied Gyb, the cat, in the milk pan. When she returned her needle was gone. Around the loss of the needle the author develops a play of farcical comedy, which has at the same time a rough, native realism. The play has a crudity which may limit its attractiveness to modern audiences, but the pictures of rural life are genuine enough, and Hodge has lived down the centuries as the type of village labourer. Meanwhile in *Supposes* (1566) George Gascoigne, basing himself on Ariosto's comedy of intrigue *I Suppositi*, wrote the first prose comedy in English, and so gained a new liberty of form for the comic drama.

Such were the beginnings of tragedy, the history play and comedy. Meanwhile there had been important developments in the ways in which plays were produced. The early, medieval drama had been performed by the guilds and was the work of amateurs, though presumably they had someone as producer who approached to being a professional. Such performances continued long after the professional theatre had been established, and there must have been several types of performer between the amateurs and the regular theatre. In medieval times the choir boys were associated with the burlesque ceremony of the boy-bishop, and possibly they were also used seriously in the liturgical plays. By the sixteenth century the choir boys under their master were engaged in the performance of regular plays. Very early in the sixteenth century the Children of the Royal Chapel were engaged in performing a play. Gradually the children of St. Paul's and of the Royal Chapel were organised into what amounted to regular professional companies. The children of schools also gave plays. Later the regular companies of children acted at times in competition with the male professional companies of adult players. There are echoes of rivalry between the boy companies and the adult actors in Elizabethan drama, notably in *Hamlet* (II. 2): 'Nay their endeavour keeps in the wonted pace, but there is, sir, an eyrie of children, little eyases, that cry out on the top of question and are most tyranically clapp'd for it'. The child companies were involved in the great quarrel of the actors in the early seventeenth century. They acted a number of Ben Jonson's plays, and in 1601 they performed *The Poetaster*, Ben Jonson's satire on the contemporary stage. This called forth Dekker's reply, *The Satiromastix*. Jonson's list of *dramatis personae* includes Salathiel Pavy, the boy player, on whose death he wrote one of his most charming lyrics.

The professional theatre throughout the Elizabethan period was affected by the attacks of the Puritans. If its complex history is to be briefly summarised it can be described as an existence in which the open hostility of the city authorities with a Puritan bias is met by the support, genuine though never vigorously expressed, of the aristocracy and the Court. The Puritans were not much concerned with drama at the Universities and the Inns of Court, or with performances at the Court itself. But they met with persistent hostility the growth of a professional theatre, basing their attack, first on the fact that plays were performed on the Sabbath, and secondly that the theatre was a centre of immorality.

When Elizabeth came to the throne there was an act against vagabonds, that is against any man without a craft. An actor was legally a vagabond unless he was attached as a retainer to a man of quality. Each of the Elizabethan companies therefore carried the name of some nobleman, such as 'the Earl of Leicester's men', in order to give themselves legal existence. This to some extent protected the actor, but it did not protect the theatre and the play. The main control lay in the country with the Justices of the Peace, and in London with the municipalities. Under Henry VIII, the central authority intervened mainly to suppress sedition and ecclesiastical heresy. Elizabeth, on the whole, was prepared to leave things to the municipalities, and these were goaded by the Puritans and by preachers not so much to license plays as to suppress them. The main excuse was the fear of plague. Efforts were made to make performances in London impossible, to which the players replied by moving to the suburbs, so that London's first theatres were built outside the city walls. In this way the corporations were out-manoeuvred, but the Puritans persisted in their attack. They wished still stricter regulations in the city, and further they wished the city to enforce the suburban magistrates to stop plays. At length the court, possibly through the influence of the great noblemen, made its influence felt and in 1581 the Master of the Revels was given a general censorship of plays. The corporations and the Puritans continued their attack, but not so violently. As Sir Edmund Chambers has written: 'the palace was the point of vantage from which the stage won its way against the linked opposition of an alienated pulpit and an alienated municipality to an ultimate entrenchment of economic independence'.

Under such conditions the drama of Shakespeare and his predecessors developed. It is indeed amazing to see how a company such as that of the Lord Chamberlain's Men, to which Shakespeare was attached, continued to develop. In 1590 it had no theatre of its own but performed in one of the London inns or in a hired theatre, but it acquired a public theatre at the Globe, and a private theatre at Blackfriars, nearer to the Court at Westminster. The Globe Theatre was rebuilt in 1599 and Shakespeare was one of the partners in the venture. The private theatre was entirely enclosed and its stage would permit of elaborate scenic effects.

When Elizabeth began her reign she was only twenty-five. She enjoyed plays and pageantry and the courtly chivalry of the tilt-yard, all, if possible, at other people's expense. There would be special performances in the banqueting-room of one of the palaces, usually between November and February, and especially at the Twelfth Night revels. Under Charles I's reign conditions had so developed that in 1634 his Queen could attend a play at Blackfriars. This was a great change from the days when the players, scarce owning a legal status, and with no centre of their own, were struggling against the Puritans.

4

Early Elizabethan Tragedy – Thomas Kyd and Christopher Marlowe

THOMAS KYD, one of the shadowy figures of the pre-Shakespearian period, was the author of *The Spanish Tragedy*, among the most popular and effective of the early tragedies. It may indeed be the earliest tragedy in England in which the Senecan motives have been made theatrically effective in a play intelligible to a general audience. Written possibly as early as 1587 it went through a number of editions. Its plot depends on a revenge theme, with a number of the motives used in *Hamlet*, including a ghost and a play within a play. The central motive is the revenge of Hieronimo, marshal of Spain, for the murder of his son Horatio. The problem for the dramatist, as in *Hamlet*, is how the interval between the murder and its discovery can be filled. This Kyd achieves by showing the moods and frenzy of Hieronimo, and by arranging theatrically effective devices for exposing the murderers. It is true that the play is melodramatic but it has a successful wildness, a romantic daring and a certainty in stage effect that made its popularity deserved.

It is probable that Kyd handled the theme of Hamlet before Shakespeare came to employ the well-known traditional story. In 1589, Thomas Nashe in a prefatory Epistle to Greene's *Menaphon* in a passage which obviously refers to Kyd, wrote: 'English *Seneca* read by candle-light yields many good sentences as "blood is a beggar" and so forth: and if you intreat him fair in a frosty morning he will afford you whole *Hamlets*, I should say handfuls of tragical speeches'. The parallels between *The Spanish Tragedy* and the Hamlet story make Kyd's authorship of a play on the theme highly probable. Some editors even maintain that the first Quarto of *Hamlet* is Shakespeare's re-working of Kyd's version. Kyd's versatility is shown by his authorship of *Cornelia* (1594), a play which is a rough translation of an academic Senecan play by the French writer Charles Garnier.

While Kyd was a skilful man of the theatre he had no great gifts of vision and poetry. These were abundantly supplied by Christopher Marlowe (1564–1593), the most mysterious of all the figures of the Elizabethan theatre; next to Shakespeare the most brilliant, and in his death the most tragic. He was educated at King's School, Canterbury, and thence he proceeded to Cambridge with a scholarship which should have led to holy orders. He took a degree but did not proceed to holy orders. He appeared in London, and he seems to have engaged in some government work, as a spy, or an agent. In 1589 a bond demanded his appearance at the next Newgate Sessions. No one knows what was his offence. In 1593 Kyd, his fellow-dramatist, was arrested for the possession of 'aetheistical' documents which he said were Marlowe's. A warrant for Marlowe's arrest followed. On 30 May 1593, Marlowe was at Eleanor Bull's tavern in Deptford with two suspicious characters named Frizer and Poley. After supper a quarrel arose over the reckoning between Frizer and Marlowe, and according to the account before the Coroner, Marlowe wounded Frizer and Frizer in return killed Marlowe. The story told in the Coroner's Court was an improbable one, and some biographers have suggested that Marlowe was the victim of a political murder.

Out of this mysterious and rather sinister background emerges the great dramatist who in a few brief years wrote *Tamburlaine*, in ten acts (possibly as early as 1586); *Dr. Faustus* (once dated about 1588, but possibly later, about 1592); *The Jew of Malta* (about 1589); *Edward II* (1592); *Dido Queen of Carthage* (1593) and *The Massacre of Paris* (1593). This genius with his burning imagination and great power over language made an outstanding contribution to English tragedy and left an influence on blank verse which has been permanent. The earlier blank verse of a play such as *Gorboduc* had little life. It was correct, but the meaning ended mechanically at the end of the line, so that to the ear it sometimes had the effect of rhyming verse without rhyme. Marlowe improved on this. He saw the necessity of running lines together until the blank verse was contained in verse paragraphs. Milton is describing the same effect when he speaks of the verse of *Paradise Lost* as 'the sense variously drawn out from one verse to another, not in the jingling sound of like endings'. Marlowe's innovation helped the young Shakespeare to discover himself in blank verse, though the later Shakespeare breaks up the verse much more than Marlowe allows himself to do. Marlowe in bringing blank verse to the service of popular tragedy endowed it with an extraordinary beauty, which reaches its height in Tamburlaine's praise of 'divine Zenocrate', or in the speeches of Faustus. He employs some of the bombastic features of Senecan verse but he endows them with an astounding sense of power. Drayton's praise of

Marlowe has a recognition of this commanding strength:
> Had in him those brave translunary things
> That the first poets had; his raptures were
> All air and fire which made his verses clear
> For that fine madness still he did retain
> Which rightly should possess a poet's brain.

Marlowe had under his control an instrument of power in which he could describe passion, pathos and the extremes of things. He lacks a verse suitable for all purposes, for lightness and wit, though there are signs in *Edward II* that before his death he was working out towards a more varied style.

While verse was his supreme attainment he added also to the conception of tragedy. He broke, partly with Seneca's aid, with the whole medieval conception in which tragedy was merely the fall of a great man. With Marlowe, as later with Shakespeare, tragedy is distress resulting from some overweening feature of weakness or strength in the character himself. In *Tamburlaine* it is a lust of power, and in *The Jew of Malta* a titanic version of avarice. In his early work Marlowe is able to bring out only one character in a play, as in Tamburlaine, or Faustus, but this he is remedying in *The Jew of Malta* and *Edward II.*

Tamburlaine is a play which modern audiences do not have an opportunity of seeing in the theatre. Based on an historical figure, the Tartar, Timur Khan, of the fourteenth century, Marlowe has built a great symbol of the quest for human power. He worked assiduously at this play and studied all the available sources. The tragedy has a certain monotony in action as one conquest follows another, but the ear is astounded by the imagery which searches out the farthest heavens to find words to describe the pleasures of earthly ambition. In *Faustus*, the problem of the plot development presented even more severe difficulties. The scene in which Faustus sells himself to Mephistopheles and the final scene of redemption are obvious and Marlowe handles them magnificently, but the manipulation of the intermediate action proved too difficult. It has been urged that Marlowe may have left some of these scenes to other hands. The theme obviously moved him strongly, as if it belonged to his own spiritual autobiography. As has been noted he had himself held a scholarship which should have led to the Church, and instead he had turned aside to activities which were sinister and to views which gave him a reputation for 'atheism'. It is possible that *Faustus* was one of Marlowe's last plays, and shows how his mind, aggressive and passionate, still occupied itself with the problem of faith and anarchy.

The Jew of Malta has not the transcendent quality of the other plays. It has intrigue, rather than grandeur, and it is governed from the first by the sinister, Elizabethan conception of Machiavelli, while in some of its scenes melodrama is allowed a licence which at times is almost grotesque. T. S. Eliot feels that it may be described as a 'savage farce' rather than as tragedy. *Edward II* is a play on which the most varied opinions have been held. Marlowe has for the first time been diverted from foreign themes to an English story, and under the influence of the chronicle play he builds this tragedy out of English history. The material which he found in Holinshed's Chronicle was not immediately promising, and though Marlowe compressed a great deal there are stretches of the play which do not avoid dullness. At the same time he clearly conceives that a play cannot be just a length of history cut off and put into the theatre. Further, he has abandoned the Tamburlaine type of character, and shown the tragedy of weakness. Nor is the action restricted to one character, but is spread more evenly over the *dramatis personae*. The brevity of Marlowe's career has a keen poignancy and his early death was an incalculable loss to English drama.

5

Early Elizabethan Comedy
and Shakespeare's other Predecessors

THERE is nothing in early Elizabethan comedy to equal
Marlowe's achievement in tragedy. The most considerable achievement is that of John Lyly (1554–1606),
though his courtly comedies are so full of contemporary
interests and fashions that they are little likely to appeal
to a modern audience. All Lyly's dramatic work lay in
comedy and his plays have a certain similarity of texture,
notably in the euphuistic dialogue, and in a use of
classical mythology partly invented, but there is variety
in design. They are all modelled for a courtly audience.
They are all in prose, except *The Woman in the Moon*,
and all of them make use of classical myth except
Mother Bombie, a comedy with realistic features.

In one group of plays Lyly works an allegory connected
with the court into a piece of classical myth. So *Sapho and
Phao* (1584) is an allegory on the courtship of Elizabeth
and the Duke of Alençon and *Endymion* (1588), the most
elaborate of the courtly allegories, presents Elizabeth as
Cynthia and Endymion as the Earl of Leicester. In *Midas*
(1589–90) the myth is more obviously used to show
Philip of Spain's grasping attempt to take England into
his power. *Campaspe*, possibly as early as 1584 and certainly one of the earliest of the plays, and one of the most
charming, is without allegory. Its plot deals with Campaspe, a captive of Alexander's with whom the painter

46

Apelles falls in love. The Emperor resigned her to Apelles, and Lyly strengthens this slight romantic plot with a number of episodes. *Gallathaea* (1588) shows Lyly's ingenuity, for he uses a tragic, classical myth and so re-designs it that it becomes a charming and ingenious device. The *Woman in the Moon* (1597), one of the most delightful of Lyly's plays, is in blank verse and free from the euphuistic elements which occupy such a large place in the prose plays. In contrast to these allegorical and classical plays Lyly wrote in *Mother Bombie* (1589–90) a Terentian comedy with a clever mixture of situations between parents and children.

Lyly pleased the courtly audience to which his comedies were addressed: it was the same audience that had welcomed his novel, *Euphues* (1579), with its elaborately balanced prose and its ingenious alliteration. So topical was he, so neatly adjusted to his age, that much of the light and colour has now disappeared. Shakespeare obviously knew his work and benefited from his study. He soon outgrew the clever euphuistic prose, but in the early plays he was deeply under its influence. His comedies, though at once more romantic and human than Lyly's, retain his ingenuity. Further, in some more detailed ways Lyly's example was potent. Particularly do the witty servants of Lyly reappear in Shakespeare's comedies.

If Lyly has ingenuity and consistency, Robert Greene (1560–92) though more unequal, commands attention at times in an engaging way. As frequently with the Elizabethan dramatists biographical material is scanty. Greene went to St. John's College, Cambridge, where he met Nashe, and after taking a degree he travelled extensively on the Continent. He returned demoralized though in a sentimental and self-pitying way he had a temporary and elaborate repentance. By 1580 he had begun a career as a writer and the rest of his life was spent in the underworld of Elizabethan literature, which had its own strange contacts with the Court and where, however incredibly, great work was produced.

At first he wrote mainly pamphlets and novels. After Marlowe's *Tamburlaine* he tried, feebly it must be admitted, an imitation entitled *Alphonsus* (1588–91). His second play, and a very strange one, was written with Lodge and entitled *The Looking Glass for London and England* (about 1590): it is a mixture of elements from the Moralities and the Miracles and modern Elizabethan satire. *Orlando* (printed in 1594) was written after Greene had read Sir John Harington's translation of Ariosto. The play is ineffective. Then there followed *Friar Bacon and Friar Bungay* (possibly 1591) and *James IV* (earlier than 1594). Of these *Friar Bacon and Friar Bungay* is outstanding. The material seems a mixture of many traditions, of *Tamburlaine* and *Faustus* in the verse, and of *Faustus* again in the pranks and devices of the action, and with an odd, unhistorical history, as if in some acknowledgement to the growing tradition of the history play. But out and beyond these, not derived but created by Greene, is the drama of the English scene, with Margaret, the country girl, all English, despite the fact that she uses classical quotations, as its centre. This is different from the native elements in the miracle plays and in *Gammer Gurton's Needle*. It is romanticised, idealised and yet made real with the milk pails, the fairings and the ale. Further, Greene has devised ways of keeping the whole play together, the court and the countryside and the world of necromancy. Out of much that was hurried and ineffective in his drama there had emerged something new, whose warm attractiveness is to be found again in Shakespeare's comedies. *James IV* also shows far more skill than Greene's earlier plays and again he achieves an original effect by combining several types of action within a single plot. The story is originally taken from Cinthio, from whom Shakespeare derived the plot of *Othello*, but it is softened, made romantic and transferred to Scotland where it is given a pseudo-historical setting. To this are added fairy interludes of Oberon, King of the Fairies, and of Bohan, a cynical, disillusioned figure well enough contrived for Shakespeare to gather suggestions here for *A Midsummer Night's Dream*, and for Jaques in *As You Like It*.

Among the other predecessors of Shakespeare a definite place, both as poet and dramatist, must be assigned to George Peele (1558–1597). In his *Arraignment of Paris* (printed 1584) he follows Lyly in employing classical myth freely for courtly purposes. Through the Paris and Oenone story he contrives to show that Elizabeth is fairer than all the goddesses. *Edward I* (printed 1593) was his ineffective experiment in history, from which he turned to the extravagant romantic tragedy *The Battle of Alcazar* (performed about 1590). In *David and the Fair Bethsabe* (about 1593) Peele returns to the early tradition of the dramatic employment of a religious theme, but the play has little to commend it though the verse is effective. By far the most original of Peele's plays was *The Old Wives' Tale* performed about 1592 in which Milton found some suggestions for *Comus*. The play opens with a realistic, contemporary, rustic scene in which Madge, the old wife, begins to tell a tale, making several false starts. She breaks off as the actors enter to perform the story she is narrating. In contrast to the homely realism of the opening the tale is romantic and extravagant. Two brothers are seeking their sister, who is in the power of a magician. It is difficult to believe that Peele is wholly serious in this part of the play, yet the treatment is not designed in caricature. We are reminded that it is Madge's mind which is being dramatically presented.

6

Shakespeare

IT IS difficult to say anything profitably of William Shakespeare (1564–1616) within the compass of one brief chapter. A library, rather too large, has already been written about his work. Here, such space as is available is devoted solely to the plays.* His earliest extant work is in the Henry VI plays (Parts I, II, and III). Of these *I Henry VI* (Folio version only), has some scenes by Shakespeare, the Temple Garden scene and certain of the Talbot scenes, but much of the rest is by other hands. Thus, as far as is known, he began his work as a practical dramatist in the native tradition of the English history play. It was to that form that he devoted a major part of his work as a dramatist, and from it there developed, by practice rather than from theoretical preconception, his idea of tragedy. *II and III Henry VI*, which appear in the Folio, exist in Quarto versions as *The Contention betwixt the two famous houses of York and Lancaster*; the text in these versions differs widely from the Folio. Since Malone's work on the text it had been, until recently, a tradition to consider that the Folio represented Shakespeare's revision of work by less competent contemporaries. The theory is improbable, for it is doubtful whether

* The reader is reminded that 'Quarto' refers to an edition of a single play, and that 'Folio' refers to a collection of the plays in one volume. Unless otherwise stated 'Folio', in this chapter, refers to the 'First Folio' published in 1623.

a very young dramatist, as yet untried, would be assigned such a task. It is more likely that the Quarto plays represent very corrupt versions of the same plays as are found in the Folio, and that Shakespeare can be considered as their sole author.

Thus he entered into the history play and into the story of the quarrel of York and Lancaster, but he came to the story almost at its end. Later, and in more mature plays (*Richard II*, *Henry IV*, and *Henry V*), he was to go back to the beginning of that history and make of the whole a dramatic epic of England. It is a great conception, but never formally planned, yet so consistent were his views of history and his vision that the plays possess a unity of design. Instead of going from the Henry VI theme to the beginning of the story Shakespeare goes on to its end with *Richard III* (1592–3), a tragedy of the type which Marlowe had developed in *Tamburlaine*. Strong in purpose, firm in character, utterly unscrupulous and violent in action, Richard III became one of the most popular of Elizabethan dramatic figures. Six Quartos of the play were published before 1622 and there was a Folio version in 1623.

During these same early years Shakespeare had begun to write comedy. The evidence for determining the order of the comedies before *A Midsummer Night's Dream* is inadequate, and so conclusions about their chronology must be a matter of taste rather than of fact. Here, I employ the order *Love's Labour's Lost*, *The Two Gentlemen of Verona*, *The Comedy of Errors*, and *The Taming of the Shrew*. All these plays contain elements which seem to find a unity in the *Dream*.

Love's Labour's Lost (no Quarto before 1598) even if

it is not the first of the plays must be one of the earliest and as such it is a miracle. The plot, unlike that in most of Shakespeare's plays, is original. It is imaginary, but there are some references to almost contemporary French history, and much of the humour depends on topical allusions worked out in part through figures similar to those of the Italian *commedia dell' arte*. The play is one of the most astounding things that Shakespeare did. It is a sixteenth-century manners comedy, where the 'finer shades' of contemporary sentiment are subjected to the light of the comic spirit by one who is new to the stage, and almost a stranger to courtly life. Nor is the world of this play previously discoverable in the drama. Shakespeare, apparently by invention, has discovered a society sophisticated and elegant, like that in Molière or Congreve. The plot is dramatic. There is little in it that can be reduced to narrative. It is not a story plot such as *The Two Gentlemen*, and so the central theme looks thin when it is put down as narrative. The King of Navarre and three courtiers swear that they will study for a fixed period and keep away from women. The Princess of France and her ladies come to them to negotiate affairs of state. Each man breaks his vow and falls in love with a lady. In addition there are complications, mistaken discoveries, incidental entertainments, foolery. But all is made dramatic to bring out the changes of mind. The elegance is a little removed from reality, for wit and fantasy are its main qualities. Biron, who is a first sketch of Benedick, and Rosaline, an earlier Beatrice, move for a moment to reality before the close.

The central theme is the breaking of a vow, a fantastic vow it is true. Later, as John Masefield has shown, that theme of the breaking of a vow to oneself, to another person, to an idea, or to the State, is the most frequently re-worked conception in Shakespeare's plays. Many features in the play are derived from Lyly and yet the total effect is altogether different. The comedy is more lively than courtly allegory, and the language more brilliant than .euphuism. For language dominates the play. It is as if Shakespeare observed every device by which words could be the instruments of wit, or the playthings of sound and fancy. Already he is engaged in that absorbing passion for words which leads from a game played for the pleasure of throwing coloured balls into the sunlight, to the compact, twisted, allusive verbal inventions of the tragedies and of the early part of *The Winter's Tale.*

The Two Gentlemen of Verona (Folio 1623) was a romantic comedy with a story plot, perhaps Shakespeare's earliest attempt in this form. As he tells it, the story is of two friends, Proteus and Valentine; Proteus loves Julia and Valentine makes love to Julia, though unsuccessfully. The friends quarrel. After many adventures, some of them highly incredible, everything rights itself. This is a different type of play from *Love's Labour's Lost,* and if one assumes that play to have come first, then Shakespeare has now rejected the method of fantasy and the elegance and good manners of a courtly world. Here one has to judge by normal standards. Yet two of the underlying motives, as Masefield has suggested, remain the same, namely that passion is not guided or controlled by reason and that men in a state of passion are false to themselves and others. The whole is conducted in an atmosphere of exaggerated sentiment and improbable adventure which belongs not to comedy but to the medieval romances. Instead of the exposures which comedy would bring to the excesses of Valentine and the uncertainty of Proteus, these characters are presented seriously and their actions brought to an unsteady conclusion. Genuine comedy, with an atmosphere of common-sense, exists only in the 'low-figures' such as Launce.

The Comedy of Errors (Folio text 1623) is another experiment. As already suggested the order of composition of these early plays cannot be precisely defined. *The Comedy of Errors* was performed at Gray's Inn in 1594: apart from that, there is no date by which its composition can be defined. Sir Edmund Chambers considers that it precedes *Love's Labour's Lost* and *The Two Gentlemen.* The precise order is not of much importance to the critic. Whatever the order it remains clear that Shakespeare is experimenting. The play is very short, and is a well-defined attempt to employ Plautine comedy in English. He borrowed from *The Menaechmi* of Plautus of which a translation was published in 1595 and from the *Amphitruo.* Shakespeare could probably read Plautus comfortably for himself in Latin. His scene is Ephesus, and in contrast to his romantic plays he preserves a unity of time and almost of place. He gives an initial sentimental argument to a comedy which depends on the confusions which arise from the existence of two sets of twins. The result is that he has rendered into a farce of situation what might in Terence or Plautus have been a comedy dependent on comment on society and the family. The Roman comedy cannot be transferred into English and retain its social purpose, for English society has such different values.

In *The Taming of the Shrew* (Folio 1623) he turns from the mechanical farce of *The Comedy of Errors* to a vigorous and effective comedy dependent on character. The play has two plots, first the wooing of the shrew Katharina by Petruchio, and secondly the dull and dimly romantic plot of Bianca and her wooers. The *Induction* must be remembered, for it explains the values of the play. The comedy is performed before Christopher Sly, a drunken tinker, dressed up as a Lord, all of which seems to imply that it must not be taken too seriously. The mood is farcical with the wilful distortion and exaggeration of certain aspects of life and character for broadly humorous purposes. A strong-willed woman and a coarse brutal man are shown in the rough and tumble of matrimony, with the final subduing of the woman. One must allow no sentimental values to intrude, for it is Sly's play, and even apart from that, Elizabethan values are different from our own.

There followed the wonderful creation of *A Midsummer Night's Dream* (1st Quarto, 1600). The plot is apparently invented and is most ingenious. Shakespeare has retained all that he has learned from his earlier comedies and with this experience he has moved into a new world. He is away from the Italianate romance to Athens, a medieval and romantic Athens of Chaucer's *Knight's Tale*, made native by the folk-lore of the English countryside. Like Greene, but with far greater skill, he combines a number of stories in a single plot. Theseus and Hippolyta are to marry and the ceremonies give a basis to the play, which may have been designed for a wedding. Amid the fantasy and romantic excesses these two characters preserve an element of normality. For the main plot Shakespeare retains pairs of lovers as he had already used them in the earlier plays. Lysander and Demetrius both love Hermia, and Helena loves Demetrius. But they are subjected to a genuinely comic treatment which was not achieved in *The Two Gentlemen*. The confusions of the love juice and the extravagance of their sentiments show how far they depart from reason, and this same irrationality of passion is emphasised by the Titania and Bottom plot. At the conclusion the comic matter of Bottom and his friends is brought, by the performance of their play, into contact with the main action. All is made luminous by the language reaching here a quality of imagination he had not previously attained.

A Midsummer Night's Dream seems to mark a period in Shakespeare's work, for there he had captured a spirit of comedy, uniting the classical with the native, the Middle Ages with the Renaissance and gathering them into a plot which has an effortless coherence. In the period which followed he continued to write both comedy and history plays, while in *Romeo and Juliet*, and in the part-authorship at least of *Titus Andronicus*, he experimented in tragedy. *Romeo and Juliet* (completed by 1594–6, 1st Quarto, 1597) is tragedy conceived in the mood of the romantic comedies and explored in the sentiment of the *Sonnets*. It is unlike the later tragedy, for in language it is lyrical and its theme is love, while its crisis depends on accident instead of being an inescapable consequence of character. Further, there is no world behind the play, as in *Hamlet*, giving reality to the whole action. The language is throughout brilliant, though its employment, as in a few of the other plays, is self-conscious.

Of the comedies of this second period possibly the earliest is *The Merchant of Venice* (1st Quarto 1600). Justly one of the most popular of the comedies, this combines the wooing of Portia at Belmont by the choice of the caskets, a faery-motived theme, with the sinister story of the Jew's bond, secured by the forfeit of a pound of flesh. These severely contrasting motives are resolved by the skill of Portia as a lady advocate, and a touch of lightness and comedy is added at the close by the incident of the exchange of rings. To enjoy the play one must not analyse the characters too closely, for Bassanio, considered with the precision of ordinary life, is little better than a rogue. The whole action is bathed in a wash of beautiful words which, while keeping the senses alert, dulls the intelligence into accepting the values presented. Yet not completely so, for Shylock seems to refuse to be bound by these artificialities and steps out of the pretty framework of the play, a figure of almost tragic dimensions.

Much Ado (about 1599) continued in the same tradition. The action is improbable and the romantic characters are unreal if brought out of the world of fine sentiment and fair language to which they belong. In the critics of romantic sentiment, in Benedick and Beatrice, Shakespeare gives a depth and penetration of character stronger than anything in the play. Upon the general mood of light-heartedness Don John is permitted to intrude an episode of tragedy, but the audience need not be genuinely fearful that he, a villain who can be exposed by Dogberry, will be ultimately successful. In *As You Like It* (1599–1600) Shakespeare seemed to gather all that he had learned in romantic comedy and to employ it in a play strong in native atmosphere, by exposing all the forms of melancholy and mood to which the mind is subject. Its gaiety, strongly contrasting with its reflective moments, the happy variety of scene, and the many firmly defined characters, Jaques, the Duke, Rosalind and Touchstone, have made it one of the most popular of all the plays. Deliberately careless in detail, it has some confident strength of structure on which it moves buoyantly along. Finally in *Twelfth Night* (about 1600) Shakespeare brought romantic comedy to a new perfection. To some modern spectators, and I am one of them, *A Midsummer Night's Dream* is the more delightful play; especially do I prefer Bottom and his men, unless their pranks are over-played, to Sir Toby Belch and his senseless crew. But even despite such personal prejudices, nothing can obscure the charm and unity of conception in this play where love in all its gentler moods of sentiment is explored and its kindliness and hypocrisy at once revealed. The characterisation is firmer than that of the *Dream* and in Malvolio, a 'humorous' character that must have delighted Ben Jonson, Shakespeare exposed self-conceit with a satiric firmness, so that the conclusion seems almost excessive to the light delicacy of the treatment as a whole.

Within these years in which Shakespeare had matured his idea of romantic comedy, he had also moved forward in his development of history play and tragedy. Already as early as 1596 he had completed the tragedy of *Romeo and Juliet*. As already noted in this popular play he carried the theme of the comedies into a tragic setting, and exploited the imagery and language which he was employing possibly at the same period in the sonnets. The catastrophe depended less on character and more on incident than in the later tragedies. In them he would give more completely an impression that the action was not merely a story, but arose out of a world whose values and atmosphere are imaged in the verse. *Romeo and Juliet* stands brilliantly apart from his main achievement of those years, which lies in the history play.

By 1596 he had written *King John* (Folio, 1623), a play which, though it may have some unsatisfactory features, is vital in Shakespeare's development and lies midway between the chronicle play and tragedy. The plot is derived from the earlier play of the *Troublesome Raigne*, so it cannot be examined as if it were Shakespeare's own. In design it lacks unity in attempting to bring together the widely separated themes of French and English antagonism, the murder of Arthur, the revolt in England and the papal plot. All this amorphous multiplicity of action seems to lead back to the diffuse methods of *Henry VI*, but the characters are now far more strongly presented and Shakespeare himself seems feeling his way through to some new conception. He has so developed the character of the Bastard Falconbridge, that he is a new creation, linking the perplexingly diverse movements of the plot, and at the same time, by his rough independence of mind, acting as a commentary, comic, satiric, and eloquent in turn, on all the values that the play suggests. Through Falconbridge Shakespeare was seeing his way to Falstaff, even to Hamlet and to the very original conception of the history play which appeared with *I and II Henry IV* and *Henry V*. The Bastard sees clearly through the pretence of chivalry in those around him. Life he knows to be a deceit, for he was born by a deceit, so he will judge not by accepted standards, but by life as he sees it, and he will act for his own purpose, which is England. Falstaff also saw through life, but his conclusion was self-indulgence and a comic egoism. The Bastard sees through everything but clings to a faith in England. He has a closely-worked intellectual consistency which is not always recognised and from its creation Shakespeare learned much that he was to use later.

King John led on the one hand to tragedy and on the other to the supreme maturing of the history plays in *I* and *II Henry IV* (Quartos 1598 and 1600). The two parts unite into a single drama, which is not tragedy but some separate mood, satiric or even comic in the most profound sense of the term. The play is a solemn reflection on civil commotion, of whose dangers Shakespeare was acutely aware, and the comic sub-plot with its satire on the methods of warfare is brought into close unity with the whole design. The characters are depicted with a superb clarity, especially in the contrast of Hotspur and the Prince. In this theme of English history Shakespeare has placed Falstaff, who, next to Hamlet, is the most discussed character in the plays. At his simplest he is a buffoon, a laughter-creating rascal, but he is more sinister, more profound, and in the second part, capable even of poignancy, as some ageing wreck of great abilities misspent. Laughter dominates, but through the laughter there peeps almost everything else from philosophy to sentiment. This great play was followed by *Henry V* (1599, Quarto 1600) which is an emblazoned and glorying exposition of war. With *Henry V* Shakespeare's work in the English history plays ends, except for that elaborate piece of pageantry *Henry VIII* of which he was part author.

From English history he had moved with great success to a Roman theme in *Julius Caesar* (1599, Folio 1623). The plot avoids the episodical matter which the English history plays even at their best possess, and instead there is a concentration on the central theme marking development of the conception of tragedy. From North's *Plutarch* he derived not only the theme but a richer model for language than Holinshed could offer. The single plot on which he concentrated, namely the struggle of the conspirators against a tyrant, offered technical difficulties, for the tyrant was killed half-way through the play. In part this finds compensation in the idea that the rebellion is not against Caesar but against Caesarism, and the ghost helps to emphasise this. The characters are as clearly defined as in *Henry IV* with the same use of contrast, as Cassius and Brutus and Antony are posed one against the other. It is on Brutus that Shakespeare concentrates, portraying there a philosophical type, treated elsewhere comically in Falstaff, and seriously in Henry VI, and in varying moods in Richard II and later in Hamlet.

Julius Caesar is in many ways the prelude to the great tragedies, but there occur in this same period three of the most puzzling and yet interesting plays in his work. These are *All's Well That Ends Well* (1601–2: Folio, 1623), *Troilus and Cressida* (1602, Quarto 1609: in the Folio, 1623 the play is called a 'tragedy'), and *Measure for Measure* (1604: Folio, 1623). *All's Well* and *Measure for Measure* are comedies developed in the mood of the tragedies. The vessel of romantic comedy is being forced to hold a burden of thought beyond its strength. The two plays have a similarity of plot. In each a man is faithless and a woman faithful. In each a woman is substituted or disguised as another in the performance of the sexual act, and so regains the faithless man. All this is worked out in a distress of spirit which penetrates beyond the story which holds the theme. The mood in the main plot is fierce, and the comic world of the sub-plot has a bawdiness and grossness not paralleled elsewhere in Shakespeare. The comedies have been described as 'dark', and as the product of a cynical mood. Yet this is not just, for a number of touches show a tenderness and charity, a faith in humanity even amid the faithlessness and obscenity of individual men. *Troilus and Cressida* puzzled the early editors, and has remained a puzzle ever since. Like *King John* it is a play in which Shakespeare is breaking through to a new dramatic vision. At times, as in Ulysses's speech on 'degree', it has some of the most illuminating passages that he wrote, and its intellectual appeal remains very strong. Yet one feels in seeing it that part of the clue to its composition and intention is missing. Clearly Shakespeare began with the medieval story of Troilus and Cressida as it was found in Chaucer and gradually became absorbed with the fact that this theme was only a late accretion onto the great Homeric legend of the *Iliad*. Chapman's translation may have helped to that change of emphasis, as indeed Shakespeare's dislike for the Greeks as compared with the Trojans may be linked with some motive of satirising Chapman. As it is Shakespeare begins with the Troilus and Cressida story and becomes involved, and indeed more interested, in the Achilles and Ajax theme. The Cressida story he found frustrating. If the lady is to be treated with any sympathy her career must be related in the values of honour as understood in the medieval courts of love. Once moral considerations dominate, and the seriousness of tragedy intrudes, Cressida becomes a wanton. Thus while the play never consolidates into a theme whose every motion is intelligible it has a fascinating brilliance, as if it belonged to a world consistent with itself but all seen in a strange light.

There followed the great succession of tragedies which are Shakespeare's supreme achievement in drama: *Hamlet* (1601: printed First Quarto 1603 and Second Quarto 1604); *Othello* (1604; Quarto, 1622); *Macbeth* (before 1606; Folio, 1623), *King Lear* (1605; Quarto, 1608); *Antony and Cleopatra* (1606; Folio, 1623); *Coriolanus* (about 1606; Folio, 1623). He had also some share in *Titus Andronicus*, *Timon of Athens* and *Pericles*. The tragedies have a sufficient number of features in common to support the conclusion that Shakespeare from his long practice in the history plays had matured a conception of tragedy which though never governed by any theoretical considerations was gaining a certain precision in design. The protagonist was a man, and one who as king, prince, or leader involved a whole people by his actions; so that at any moment his personal conduct might become part of the 'world's debate'. Each possessed a great nature and outstanding gifts and yet had some weakness or corruption which made him unequal to the situation with which he was faced. How deeply Shakespeare contemplated this conception of character can be seen from a complex and revealing passage in *Hamlet* (I, iv. 23-36):

> So, oft it chances in particular men,
> That for some vicious mole of nature in them,
> As, in their birth—wherein they are not guilty

Since nature cannot choose his origin—
By their o'er growth of some complexion,
Oft breaking down the pales and forts of reason,
Or by some habit that too much o'er-leavens
The form of plausive manners; that these men—
Carrying, I say, the stamp of one defect,
Being nature's livery, or fortune's star,—
His virtues else—be they as pure as grace,—
As infinite as man may undergo—
Shall in the general censure take corruption
From that particular fault.

The love interest dominant in the comedies becomes now
of minor importance, and only in *Antony and Cleopatra*
does it remain the main motive of the action. Comedy,
though retained, is given a subsidiary place and is worked
into subtle, even poignant contrast with the main action
as in *Hamlet* and *King Lear*. Language, particularly in
the use of imagery, gains an enhanced power, so that each
of these plays has its own world of symbols and of verbal
associations that serve as an imaginative accompaniment
to the action. Above all, each theme seems to take place
within a world so consistent with itself and so familiar,
that criticism has often been in danger of treating the
characters as human figures with lives independent of the
immediate action. Each play is able to appeal at a number
of different levels. The theme is in one sense so obvious,
and the characters so clear, and the incident so strong
and active, that anyone interested in human life will be
moved. But accompanying this there is a range of suggestion in the language and there is subtlety in the characters
which endless exploration never seems finally to exhaust.

Despite these similarities, the tragedies are very different. *Hamlet*, on which criticism has already said too much.

C-ED

is the play with the greatest multiplicity of appeal. In this Renaissance world, art, literary criticism, the elegances of language and the speculations of philosophy, all have place along with the high tragic movement, so that satire, comedy, ironic comment, and moral reflection mingle with death, madness, suicide and revenge. In contrast *Othello* has a simplicity in language, and an atmosphere and theme more domestic than is usual in the tragedies. The gain is in a supreme concentration, and though the unities of the classical tragedy are not applied, by use of 'double-time', one for the incidents and another for the action, Shakespeare gives to the play an intense singleness of purpose. In *Macbeth* he chose a character far more evil than he elsewhere employs. Yet he retains some sympathy for him, though it cannot be intellectually justified. The 'weird sisters' give to his conduct a predestined inevitability, and to these supernatural promptings must be added the goadings of Lady Macbeth. The more evil he becomes the more does he evolve some strange pathos in his isolation. For the image of his own evil haunts him like a fever, and his poetic power, supreme among the tragic heroes, permits him to portray the symbols of self-torment with which he is afflicted. *Macbeth* is the tragedy of a brave mind diseased by ambition. *King Lear* shows the more normal decay of a proud, impassioned nature by the inroads of old age and senility. While *Othello* is the more compact *King Lear* is the most extended of the tragedies, with an epic scale, and in the storm scenes a wild symbolical movement develops that seems to reach beyond any precise location of place and time. The fierce, tormented action, unremitting in its solution, is the most stark and harrowing of the plays and stretches the capacity of both actor and producer more than any other of the tragedies. *Antony and Cleopatra* stands a little apart. Love has returned as a major theme and the woman is given a role equal at least to that of the male protagonist. So widespread are the scenes and so numerous that it would seem at first that Shakespeare was returning to the method of the history plays. But it is not so. For with the aid of Plutarch he has seized on this great theme of Antony's passion and of Cleopatra's 'infinite variety' and in language patterned with rich beauty, abundantly endowed with magnificence and power, he has contrived an action moving and original, whose full force must be discovered in the theatre and not from the printed pages of a book. *Coriolanus*, again a Roman theme from Plutarch, is in severe contrast, though both deal with men of action rather than with self-tortured figures such as Brutus, Othello, Macbeth and Lear. *Antony and Cleopatra* is spacious and full of glamour, *Coriolanus* confined as if the whole play were one continuous argument. Antony's fault is human and close to ordinary human motives, but Coriolanus endures a pride which is a specialized emotion. The spectator can identify himself with Hamlet and Antony, but he has to watch Coriolanus. Even then his motives are discovered mainly through the conduct and the speeches of others. The verse has a severity which is deliberate, but seems restricted and colourless in comparison with that of some of the earlier tragedies. The division of the action over the play is novel and interesting, for it begins with the bustle of a chronicle play and ends like a Greek tragedy.

The motive of reconciliation which struggles with tragic

destiny in *Lear* and *Coriolanus* becomes supreme in the last plays: *Cymbeline* (1609; Folio, 1623); *The Winter's Tale* (about 1610; Folio, 1623) and *The Tempest* (1611; Folio, 1623). In *Cymbeline* Shakespeare submitted to the influence of Beaumont and Fletcher. The play has a large pattern of incident but little depth of character portrayal. The main motive is not unlike that in *King Lear:* a daughter, Imogen, offends her father Cymbeline, but now a reconciliation is permitted and only the wicked elements are destroyed. Although the pattern of incident is elaborate, one is not conscious, as in the great tragedies, of a world behind the story. The skill lies rather in the control of the complex plot and particularly in its resolution in the fifth act. Throughout, the play seems full of echoes, especially in the motives for action: Cymbeline in his anger is reminiscent of Lear; the distrust of Imogen's virtue recalls *Othello*; the despair of Posthumus sends the spectator back to *Troilus and Cressida*, and the deceit of Iachimo to the so-called 'dark' comedies. It seems a transition play, full of charm and ingenuity, but lacking the uniqueness of vision and the strenuousness in its pursuit of the great tragedies.

So with two comedies, very different in design but similar in motive, the plays come to an end. In the Folio of 1623 one of them, *The Tempest*, stood first and the other, *The Winter's Tale*, stood last. *The Winter's Tale* opens in the mood of the tragedies, and in the crowded and elliptical lines of Leontes explores again the Othello theme of jealousy. Then suddenly the mood relaxes. The change comes precipitously in a stage-direction: 'Exit Antigonus chased by a bear: Enter a Shepherd'. With the Shepherd's entry romance and comedy and reconciliation return, and remain to the end. The rural and pastoral scenes with which the play closes are happily portrayed, and in Autolycus a new character is added to Shakespeare's comic figures. Critics have commented on the irregularity of the construction and the improbability of the theme. Of all this Shakespeare was aware as his Chorus of Time shows, but on the stage the whole finds unity in a strange delight, not realistic certainly, but with a soft mellow quality of its own. *The Tempest* is either the last of the plays or an early play revised later for some special occasion. It is known to have been performed in 1613 for the celebration of the wedding of the Elector Palatine and Princess Elizabeth. It differs from all the previous comedies. Like *A Midsummer's Night Dream* it is regular in form and has a close unity of theme. Many of the characters, unlike those elsewhere in Shakespeare, seem abstractions, and of these Caliban is a profound conception, based in part on his reading of Montaigne and of the voyages of discovery. The play uses the machinery and stage device which performance in a private theatre or at court would permit, and ends with Prospero's speech which seems like Shakespeare's own farewell to the stage. It is a play never supremely success-ful on the modern stage, but infinitely full of suggestion and meaning as if the whole of life were somehow symbolised within it. Emile Montegut commenting on the fact that *The Tempest* appeared first in the 'Folio' wrote: 'Like the emblematic frontispieces of antique books it prepares the reader for the substance of all that follows. No other play will do this, none other is a synthesis of all.'

7

Shakespeare's Contemporaries –
Ben Jonson – Thomas Dekker – Domestic Drama
John Heywood – George Chapman

OUTSTANDING among Shakespeare's contemporaries was Ben Jonson (1572–1637), a writer of two learned tragedies, *Sejanus* and *Catiline*, and of many individual and original 'humours' comedies. The contrasts between Shakespeare and Ben Jonson are marked and obvious. In *Hamlet*, Polonius who, whatever his defects, was a learned critic of the drama, said that a play was composed either on 'the law of writ' or 'the liberty'. This shows that Shakespeare knew all the talk about the 'unities' and the classical rules. Indeed there is a great deal of theoretical dramatic criticism in his plays, and *Hamlet* is full of it. Shakespeare, however, was not bound by the 'rules' when he entered his own dramatic workshop. He based his construction on 'the liberty' of his own imagination. To Ben Jonson the 'rules' are not merely practical precepts, to be used if convenient, but dictates founded on Olympus which every good man must follow. Though often forced by the necessities of the theatre and by concessions to his audiences to modify his ideal, he aims at a pattern which shall follow the ancients and preserve the 'unities'. As he writes in the prologue to *Volpone*:

> The laws of time, place, persons, he observeth,
> From no needful rule he swerveth.

Each play shall have one action, played in one scene,

within the period of one day: such was the ideal. Jonson insists that the audience shall realise how clever he has been in his regular and original compositions, and in his prefaces and comments he hectors his readers into appreciating how cunningly he has constructed his plays. He is like some dowager insisting that all shall appreciate her ungainly daughters, though Jonson's dramatic daughters were far from ungainly.

Part of Jonson's originality is that he brings the scene of comedy from Italy, where Shakespeare had placed it, and normally sets his vigorous themes, with the notable exception of *Volpone,* in contemporary England. He did not at once achieve this increase in realism, for the first version of *Every Man in His Humour* has its scene in Italy, and only in the Folio version of 1616 do the characters appear with English names and on an English background. To this presentation of contemporary life he brought a definite theory of comedy based on the 'humours'. This conception was partly Latin, partly medieval, and in part an Elizabethan fashion. In Latin comedy each character belonged to a recognisable type, and maintained throughout certain well-defined attributes. This static conception of character Jonson maintained and re-affirmed by adapting the medieval belief that temperament was governed by an excess of one of the four 'humours', hot, cold, moist and dry. In Elizabethan times this medieval physiology was not treated with complete seriousness, but its vocabulary became a popular fashion in sophisticated conversation and this again Jonson exploited. The result in the plays is that one quality was affixed to each character and this was exposed in the action. It gave to Jonson's figures a strong though static quality with often a satiric mood dominant.

Chronologically Jonson's comedies are divided by his two tragedies. The earliest group precedes *Sejanus* (acted 1603). The middle group includes the great comedies, *Volpone* (1606); *The Silent Woman* (1609); and *The Alchemist* (1610). These lie between *Sejanus* and *Catiline* (1611). Then follow the last comedies beginning with *Bartholomew Fair* (1614).

The earliest of the 'humours' plays, *Every Man in His Humour* (acted 1598, Quarto 1601 and revised version in the Folio 1616), is a theatrically effective play. A simple and original plot permits the dramatic exposure of a number of characters: the elder Knowell, the stern father; Kitely, the jealous husband; and Bobadill the braggart soldier who is the outstanding portrait. There followed *Every Man Out of His Humour* (acted 1599, Quarto 1600), which is preluded by an open declaration of the aim of 'humours' comedy and of its intention of stripping 'the ragged follies of the time'. A deepening satiric mood leads to the presentation of a gallery of 'humours' figures presented with some bitterness. The play has no central theme except that Macilente exposed the weaknesses of the characters and in turn has his own envy exposed. One of Jonson's most able critics, Miss Ellis-Fermor, has suggested that he had in his temperament a 'non-dramatic' element, and that in some plays of this period he 'imposed dramatic form upon his own recalcitrant imagination'. Such would certainly seem to be true of *Cynthia's Revels* (acted 1600, Quarto 1601), in which masque and myth mingle with contemporary satire. Of the same type, though more firmly constructed, was *The Poetaster* (acted 1601, Quarto 1602), where the Roman

scene is applied to the exposure of the complicated rival-
ries of the Elizabethan dramatists, particularly in an
attack on Dekker and Marston. The play was not popular
with audiences in the theatre and so Jonson determined
to leave comedy for tragedy:

> Since the Comic Muse
> Hath prov'd so ominous, I will try
> If Tragedy hath a more kind aspect.

In *Sejanus* (acted 1603, Quarto 1605), he designed a
learned Roman tragedy on the factual record of history
as found in the *Annals* of Tacitus and in Juvenal's satire.
Hazlitt called it 'a mosaic of translated bits', but less than
a quarter is actual translation. Though Jonson respects
the Unities he modifies them in order to keep closer to
history, and from an attempt to compromise between the
classical drama of Seneca and the known desires of his
audiences. Shakespeare had by this time written *Julius
Caesar*, and possibly Jonson was attempting to compete
in his own conscientious and factually accurate way with
the Shakespearian picture of the Roman world which
ignored detail but remained living and dynamic, and
proved very popular. In essence it was tragedy on the old
medieval theme of the fall of the proud man. Its characterisation was static as in the comedies, and indeed seemed
in a way a 'humours' conception elevated to a tragic
scale. Had he maintained this central dramatic theme he
could have attained success, but the action was complicated by some forty characters, and as Dr. Boas has said
he turned to a mass of classical sources and 'became
entangled in intricate historical issues unfamiliar to Globe
audiences'.

There followed the three great comedies. Of these

Volpone (acted 1606, Quarto 1607), is the comedy of the author of *Sejanus*. It has a grim outline sometimes reminiscent of tragedy. This magnificent play has captured audiences whenever it has been competently revived. The theme is of Volpone, a man of seeming virtue who enjoys roguery, and by a consuming avarice has gathered riches which Tamburlaine might have envied. So he salutes his gold as if here were the supreme earthly felicity:

> Open the shrine that I may see my saint,
> Hail the world's soul and mine.

The follies of the other characters are shown in the various ways in which they seek legacies from Volpone. The main agent of the action is Mosca, the cunning servant of Roman comedy, developed almost beyond recognition. The plot structure has a masterly simplicity, and the transference of the scene from London to Venice seems to symbolise that the comic mood has darkened since the composition of the early plays, and that their author now sees his characters as bitter children in a life which is pathological and diseased. In *The Silent Woman* (acted 1609), Jonson returned to something approaching comedy in the more gay sense of the word. The play has farcical elements such as the marriage of a recluse to a talkative person in the belief that she is silent, and the later discovery that the marriage is a trick and the 'silent woman' a boy. The sudden dénouement seems to have displeased contemporary audiences, and this, the happiest and most farcical of Jonson's comedies, was not an immediate success. Dryden and Samuel Pepys were later to enjoy the play, which indeed has something of the elegance of the 'manners' comedy cultivated in the Restoration period.

In *The Alchemist* (acted 1610, Quarto 1612), Jonson achieved the neatest and possibly the best of all his comedies. The play shows three rogues, Subtle, Face and Doll, in possession of the house of Lovewit, who has left London on account of the plague. They pretend to powers of alchemy and magic, and so expose the greed and pretence of a number of clients. The play, which opens vigorously with one of the finest rows in Elizabethan literature, works up to a crescendo which is brought to a more genial conclusion than is usual in Jonson's comedy.

From this period of mature comedy Jonson returned to Senecan tragedy in *Catiline*, a more severe play than *Sejanus* and one that by the end of the second act had lost the interest of contemporary audiences. Yet that the play attracted wide attention is seen from its frequent reproduction, and Jonson himself regarded it as his best achievement in this kind. The tragedy's prospects of success were frustrated by Cicero's very long speech in the fourth act. Jonson is now making the minimum concession to popular taste and, as if he despaired of his audiences, he followed his own conception of Senecan tragedy more rigorously than in *Sejanus*. He introduces the play with a Ghost, and he employs choruses between the acts. This rigidity in design combined with his excessive loyalty to the details of Sallust's accounts and of Cicero's speeches, deprives the play of theatrical effectiveness.

The comedies of Jonson's last period have had a very varied critical reception, but it is generally agreed that the first of them, *Bartholomew Fair* (acted 1614, Quarto 1631), was one of his happiest and most popular achieve-

ments. Jonson, having failed in tragedy constructed on
his own principles, seems to go on holiday. It is rather
like a seventeenth-century gallery of pictures in a
Dickensian manner, though Jonson, belonging to a less
squeamish age, is able to indulge in a realism and frank-
ness not permitted to Dickens. There is little academic
intrusion either in character study or in plot structure; the
Puritans are vigorously condemned and the low figures
of the Fair most vividly presented. Even to modern
audiences the picture still remains crowded and lively,
and for Jonson's contemporaries this portrait of Jacob-
ean London must have appealed by its keen verisimilitude.
The four comedies which follow have sometimes been
described as 'dotages'. I would only affirm a personal
opinion that I think they are far better than is usually
believed and that they should be tested on the stage, the
only place where a play can be fairly judged. *The Devil
is an Ass* (acted 1616) describes the visit of a minor devil
to London, and contrives to combine some morality
material with adroit and entertaining contemporary
satire. *The Staple of News* (acted 1625), is a satire on news-
mongering and also on the technical slang and cant
language of various groups. Such is its originality and
strength that it is difficult to perceive any mental weaken-
ing in the author. *The New Inn* (acted 1629), is more unequal and was badly received on its first production.
Jonson seems to have realised that his work was almost
over, for in *The Magnetic Lady* (written 1632), he brings
his 'humours' comedy formally to an end.

Shakespeare and Jonson were obviously aware of each
other's achievement, as the prologues to *Every Man in
His Humour* and *Henry V* indicate. But apart from some

rivalry and a steady determination not to be influenced by one another they seem to have held each other in affection. Jonson is recorded as criticising Shakespeare's unlearned and rapid methods, but he paid a generous tribute on Shakespeare's death.

Apart from his plays Jonson showed his theatrical skill in the production of courtly masques. These entertainments, in which nobly-born amateurs, and sometimes royalty itself, played their graceful parts, developed in splendour under the lavishness which the Stuarts expended on the arts that pleased them. Jonson, who could fashion massive, even ponderous, tragedies, seems to have enjoyed these lighter exercises, and in their 'bodily part' he was happy in having the collaboration of Inigo Jones. Already in 1605 he had contrived the *Masque of Blackness* in which the Queen and her ladies had appeared. Throughout his career he brought classical learning, lyrical skill and great ingenuity to bear upon this artificial, courtly pleasure. The greatness of his achievement lies elsewhere, but the masques, like his odes and lyrics and his critical works, show the versatility of his mind and of his creative genius. His personality is difficult to assess, for it can pass from large and architectural design to light and graceful exercises. Out of the same mind came *Catiline*, *The Alchemist*, the masques, and that perfect miniature, the poem on Salathiel Pavy, the boy-actor.

Apart from Shakespeare no-one can compare with Jonson in range and power of creative achievement. One of those who shared something of his satiric talent is John Marston (1576–1634). Of this strange personality little is known biographically. His early work was as a satirist, but it would seem that about 1599 he began writing for the stage. Later he gave up the theatre and entered the Church. One feels that Marston's biography, if the material were available, would be a rewarding study. He brought to the drama some of the savage and satiric aggressiveness which had distinguished his verse in *The Scourge of Villany* (1598). He entered into the quarrels of the players, and he is satirised in a number of Jonson's plays.

His main work in tragedy is *Antonio and Mellida*, a play in ten parts, which was acted by 1600, published 1602. This tragedy is on a revenge theme, and it parallels at a number of points incidents and motives in the Hamlet story. Marston has the ghost of a father appearing to a son, a weak mother, a play within a play, and a melancholic view of the worthlessness of life. It has been surmised that Shakespeare was led to re-work an early Hamlet play by Kyd because a play with some elements of the theme by Marston had become popular. As a play Marston's piece will not compare with *Hamlet*, for it is undigested and theatrically unsure. But part of the conception is there and a great deal of the atmosphere. Incidentally it is of interest that Shakespeare went out of his way in *Hamlet* to discuss the controversy of the boy-players and the adult-players, and this was a matter in which Marston was deeply involved. In verse and language Marston belongs to the earlier Elizabethen tradition, and seems ever in danger of straining the verse too far. It may be that Shakespeare had some such thoughts in mind in his comments on verse in *Hamlet* in the player's speech.

Marston has one memorable comedy, *The Malcontent* (published 1604). The play is comedy only in that it avoids a tragic conclusion. Its subject is elaborate intrigue, and its story has something in common with *Measure for Measure*. A banished duke returns to his court under the name of Malevole. After watching the intrigues and immoral actions of his associates he finds an appropriate moment in which to reveal himself. He is largely a 'humours' character, and this is Marston's study of that malcontent figure found in *Othello* in Iago, and in *The Duchess of Malfi* in Bosola.

Jonson, Chapman and Marston, though they were three, very different and contending personalities, were jointly responsible in 1605 for the comedy of *Eastward Ho*. The tone of this piece is much lighter and more genial than that of the plays for which Marston was solely responsible. The play contained references to the Scottish courtiers who had streamed south with James I, and these satiric allusions led to the temporary imprisonment of the writers. *Eastward Ho* is allied to plays of the citizen type. The characters are presented in Jonson's 'humours' manner and the values are moral. But the whole is conceived more light-heartedly than in Jonson's own work. There are some excellent realistic scenes of Thames-side London in the play.

A number of writers had shared with Jonson a desire to bring drama to the English scene. Among them one of the most interesting and successful was Thomas Dekker (1572–1632). He had a long career as a dramatist, and much of his work was done in collaboration. In *Satiro-Mastix* (1602), he replied to Jonson's *Poetaster*, and here he was collaborating with Marston. *The Shoemaker's Holiday* (printed 1600), the play which is most clearly his own, has an excellently contrived contemporary setting. All the knowledge which he was to show as a prose writer in his pamphlets, such as *The Seven Deadly Sins of London* (1606), and *The Gull's Horn Book* (1609), seem present in this play. It is realistic comedy, but its mood contrasts with the moral 'humours' comedy of Jonson. A number of elements combine within it. First there is a recognisable picture of citizen life, centring in Simon Eyre, the shoemaker. This element Dekker has derived from Thomas Deloney's *The Gentle Craft*. Supporting this realistic centre of the comedy is the romantic story of Rose and Lucy. The whole is given a naïve atmosphere and a good-humoured charm. In structure it has a certain rather obvious development, but the scenes are full of effective and amusing touches, and the characterisation is strong. The play as a whole has some fresh and open geniality which has retained it a place on the stage.

More ambitious was *The Honest Whore* (Printed: Part I, 1604, and Part II, 1605), where Dekker seems to have had Middleton as a collaborator. This is an example of domestic drama with comedy elements mingled. Heywood's *A Woman Killed with Kindness*, the chief example of the type, to which reference is made below, had been published in 1603. *The Honest Whore*, like all of Dekker's work, has little strength of structure. Its quality is derived from individually effective scenes and from well-defined characters. A duke prevents his daughter, Infelice, from marrying the Prince Hippolito. Bellafronte, a harlot, makes protestation of love to Hippolito who refuses her, and she repents of the life she has led. By a ruse, at the close, Hippolito marries Infelice. In an unrelated subsidiary plot Candido, an honest citizen, endures the attacks of his shrewish wife and the pranks of the young wits. In the second part Hippolito, now married, tries to seduce Bellafronte but she repels him. In revenge he almost ruins her. The Candido comic plot is still maintained as a independent theme, nor does the author aim at unity except that he brings all the characters to Bridewell at the close. Despite all its apparent deficiencies the play has strength. Bellafronte is depicted with genuine pathos for realism and sentimentality seem to strengthen one another in her portrayal. The scenes in her house are some of the most graphic pictures of contemporary life in Elizabethan drama. This is helped in the second part by the very original conceptions of the character of Matheo, Bellafronte's worthless husband, and of Orlando Friscobaldo, her pathetically faithful father, who serves to solve the complications of the action. Dekker also composed in a less realistic manner in *Old Fortunatus* (acted before 1600), though here he is probably only a collaborator. The origin of the play is a German legend, of how Fortunatus, visited by Fortune, is allowed to have a number of his wishes. In the later acts Fortune visits the sons of Fortunatus. Both father and sons fail to please the Goddess and they die. The play has a mixture of motives, for at times it is reminiscent of the morality plays and sometimes of Marlowe's *Faustus*. Despite its formlessness it has vigour and some poetry. It appears as an example of an older style of drama living on and competing with newer and more ambitious forms. It is in very marked contrast to the realism of *The Shoemaker's Holiday*.

In the survey of Jonson and Dekker the tradition of

basing plays on contemporary and realistic scenes has already been noted. Shakespeare had chosen another way, and although his drama is thronged with contemporary figures the scene itself in the comedies is normally set outside England. In the seventeenth century both these methods had their adherents. Beaumont and Fletcher, as will appear later, were to construct a tragi-comedy and tragedy on scenes which were far removed from any contemporary reality. On the other hand a number of writers, both in comedy and in tragedy, showed the domestic scene not too far detached from the background of their audience's life.

The theme of infidelity committed in a circle where the responsibilities are solely domestic had not been a motive that interested Shakespeare, but its popularity is shown by the appearance of an early work, *Arden of Feversham* (published 1592), and attempts have been made 'to ascribe this piece to Shakespeare. A play of no exceptional merit, it yet contrives to tell clearly its story of the murder of Arden by his wife Alice because of her love for Mosbie. Much of the play is concerned with unsuccessful attempts at this murder, and the culmination lies in its execution. Up to the moment of her final, and rather unreal, repentance, Alice's character is well conceived. She is outlined as a strong personality, very certain of her hatred for her husband and of her love for Mosbie, very passionate and very direct, and a welcome contrast to the indeterminate women who appear in some of the later tragedies. A similar play of later date was *A Yorkshire Tragedy* (about 1606, printed 1608), a short piece which dealt with the Calverley murder.

The main practitioner in the form was Thomas Heywood (1575–1633). He was a prolific writer, as he himself suggested in the address to the reader in *The English Traveller* (1633), where he wrote: 'one reserved amongst two hundred and twenty, in which I have had either an entire hand or at least a main finger'. His career was typical of the dramatic journeyman working rapidly in a great variety of styles. In his preface to *The Fair Maid of the West* (1631), he spoke with contempt of the dramatists who took pains over the publication of their plays, and particularly he seemed contemptuous of Ben Jonson's elaborately prepared Folio of 1616. 'My plays,' he wrote, 'have not been exposed to the public view of the world in numerous sheets and a large volume.'

Probably the earliest of his extant plays was *The Four Prentices of London* (1600), which is one of the extravagant citizen plays attacked later by Beaumont and Fletcher in *The Knight of the Burning Pestle*. In it the crusades are adapted to citizen heroics. There followed a great variety of plays of various types, history, adventure, comedy, farce, with themes both classical and modern. Of all these hybrid pieces one of the most vigorous is *The Fair Maid of the West* (published 1631). Out of all this dramatic activity Heywood's most individual contribution remains in domestic tragedy and in the domestic problem play.

A Woman Killed with Kindness (1603, printed 1607), has all the qualities of the type. Frankford permits an impecunious friend, Wendoll, to stay in his house. Wendoll seduces Frankford's wife and this Frankford discovers. In the usual heroic or tragic drama, as in *Othello*, Frankford would have killed both his wife and her lover. Here instead, pitying his wife, he sends her to live in seclusion on one of his estates, and there she dies in his presence. Heywood is less interested in the motives which lead to the infidelity than in the results which arise from repentance. He is more occupied by Frankford's strange and morbid mercy than by the love of Wendoll and Alice. This leads to a naïve and elementary presentation of the character of Wendoll, who is made to expose himself in a series of declamatory and narrative speeches. Frankford, in contrast, is revealed with some psychological insight. Heywood from his prologue seems to be conscious that he is attempting something fresh in drama:

Look for no glorious state, our muse is bent
Upon a barren subject, a bare scene.

A much later example of the same type was *The English Traveller* (printed 1633 but probably composed much earlier). A young traveller returning home falls in love with the wife of a friend, an old man, who has been good to him. He refuses, however, to compromise the lady. Meanwhile an unfaithful young gallant seduces the wife and some of the blame attaches to the young traveller. The wife repents and dies. Again one has the impression that Heywood is not interested in giving adequate motives to the action. For him the attraction lies in the 'moral dilemma of his characters and in the sentiment aroused by the contemplation of their suffering and their repentance. With all its inadequacies Heywood had established a drama nearer to the lives and interests of many of his audience than romantic tragedy and tragi-comedy could ever be. In the decades of the seventeenth century which precede the closing of the theatre other types of drama were on the whole to be more popular, but in the eighteenth century the bourgeois interests represented by domestic drama would again prevail. In its own age it seems to belong to a different world from that of Chapman, Webster, Beaumont and Fletcher, and Tourneur.

George Chapman (1559–1634) is one of the most individual and learned of the writers for the theatre. His life was a long one, for he had in his younger days completed Marlowe's *Hero and Leander* and he had lived on to be a collaborator in the fourth decade of the seventeenth century with James Shirley. Though his major contribution lies in tragedy he was a versatile composer of comedies and had gained success with *The Blind Beggar of Alexandria* as early as 1596. How varied is his talent can be seen by comparing *The Gentleman Usher* (printed 1606), a theme of romantic tragi-comedy, and *The Old Joiner of Aldgate* (acted 1602), which is based on a sordid contemporary scandal over a marriage lawsuit. Though the play is not extant Professor Charles Sisson has established its plot from the records of legal proceedings.

Some have seen in Chapman the 'rival' poet of Shakespeare's sonnets, and it is possible that in the disputes of the players Shakespeare and Chapman found themselves on different sides. Jonson thought well of Chapman's work, particularly his masques. Indeed he considered the masques of Chapman and Fletcher as comparable with his own. Chapman was, with Jonson, the most learned of the dramatists. He is an uneven writer, but one of great energy and power. Much of his best work lay outside the drama in his translation of the *Iliad* and the *Odyssey*. He came to the drama late in his career. He was forty when he began writing comedies in 1596, and these are his main dramatic output for a decade. Earlier criticism has inclined to ignore these plays, but recently ample justice has been done to this side of his genius. He seemed capable of everything, from theatrical reportage to the comedy and romance of such a play as *Monsieur D'Olive* (published 1606). It is indeed difficult to discover in these plays the rugged powers of Chapman the translator and tragic poet.

From 1603 to 1613 there followed his career as a writer of tragedies of which the most notable are *Bussy D'Ambois* (acted 1604); *The Revenge of Bussy D'Ambois* (acted about 1611); and *The Tragedy of Byron* (acted 1608). These plays were original in conception. He employs themes derived and elaborated from nearly contemporary French history, mingling characters of his own invention with historical figures. Though he is to some extent indebted to Seneca the general design of the tragedy is neither Senecan nor Shakespearean. In *Bussy D'Ambois* he portrays the love of Bussy for the wife of Montsurry, and the death of Bussy which follows when Montsurry takes his revenge. The play had some success on the stage, mainly for the bold way in which Bussy's character is struck forth, for he has the same gesture of magnificence and ambition as is to be found in Marlowe's figures.

In *The Revenge of Bussy D'Ambois* there is a less conclusive plot based on a variation of the revenge theme. Clermont d'Ambois achieves the death of Montsurry and his own suicide. The ghost of Bussy stalks the stage, aggressively, as if he had as much right to be there as any of the living characters. *The Conspiracy and Tragedy of Byron* is a continuous piece in ten acts. The theme again follows French history. The plot, like that of *Coriolanus*, is the story of a proud and ambitious man. It is as if Chapman had looked back at the figure of Tamburlaine and contemplated the whole theme of power again, but more philosophically.

The plays of Chapman do not seem good stage plays, but as they are never seen in the modern theatre it is impossible to judge them from this, the only way that ultimately matters. Shakespeare was able to give poetry and a good stage play, for his poetry, even when most exuberant, was at the service of his drama. Chapman, like some nineteenth-century dramatists, seems to live for his poetry alone. Further his language, though magnificent, is often obscure and possesses a certain 'monotonous eloquence'. Swinburne, who writes one of his best essays on Chapman, contrasts his obscurity with that of Browning. In Browning the obscurity often arises because the poet is thinking too quickly, but Chapman's obscurity depends upon a certain confusion in his massive and original thought, 'the treasure hidden beneath the dark gulfs and crossing currents of his rocky and weedy waters'. It is difficult to believe that any audience in the theatre was able to understand the complexities of the involved and elliptical sentences in which his rhetoric is contained. Dryden, who belonged to an age that sought passionately for clarity, condemned Chapman's language as 'a dwarfish thought dressed up in gigantic words'. This is unjust, for there is a nobility in both the language and thought, a fury in the eloquence, and each idea as it arises in the author's mind seems decked and expanded by almost unending comparisons. It is as if one who possessed all the ingenuity of a metaphysical poet had determined to write verse for the theatre.

The personality revealed in the tragedies is a noble one. Chapman had a high ideal for the human mind, and this he attempted to express in tragedy. It can be found in the dedication to *The Revenge*: 'material instruction, elegant and sententious excitation to virtue and deflection from her contrary, being the soul, limbs and limits of authentical tragedy'. Chapman's view that man is capable of nobility and high-mindedness is comparable to that found in Wordsworth's *The Happy Warrior*. Against that conception of nobility his mind dwelt with the conception of power and the quest for human greatness. Though these conceptions are developed dramatically much of their treatment comes in passages which read like essays in verse. Shakespeare used that method, as in Ulysses' speech on 'degree' in *Troilus and Cressida*, but he was sparing in its employment and he attempted to relate it to the action. Chapman, guided often by memories of Seneca, Epictetus and Horace, is apt to allow philosophical reflection to take an excessive place.

Among the early seventeenth-century dramatists one of the strangest and most individual is Cyril Tourneur. Of his life little is known. He was probably born between 1570 and 1580. In the later part of his career he was involved in a number of duties which touched affairs on state at a subordinate level. He was at Cadiz on Sir Edward Cecil's unhappy expedition of 1625 and died in the next year. His reputation rests on two plays, *The Atheist's Tragedy* (published 1611), and *The Revenger's Tragedy* (acted 1607, and published in the same year though without Tourneur's name, but assigned to him in a list of plays made in 1656). In date Tourneur is a little earlier than Webster and he is before Fletcher, Ford and Shirley who are considered in the next chapter. Yet he seems by his spirit to belong to the latest mood in Stuart drama. He has something of that strange atmosphere which is to appear later in Middleton's *The Changeling*. Tourneur's mind seems pitiless, and his cruel world is one into which normality is never permitted to intrude. Unlike Webster he never relents towards his tormented characters. Dramatically and poetically *The Revenger's Tragedy* is much more able than *The Atheist's Tragedy*. A number of theories have been constructed to place *The Revenger's Tragedy* second, but there is no satisfactory evidence.

The Atheist's Tragedy opens with a brilliant first scene in which D'Amville expounds his philosophy to his instrument Borachio. His aim is to help his nephew Charlemont to the wars so that in his absence he may kill Charlemont's father and help his own sons to wealth. The plot becomes involved after this direct start, and scenes which are filled with violence and horror move in rapid succession. D'Amville finally loses his sons and is himself killed by the axe which was meant to bring Charlemont to his death. Amid all the melodrama and the terror the audience are made to feel the presence of a contemplative mind which surveys this evil world, believes in its existence, and seeks out its meaning.

The Revenger's Tragedy is a more powerful play. Professor Allardyce Nicoll, who has prepared the most satisfactory edition of Tourneur, draws attention to the excellence of the opening. Vindice, holding in his hand the skull of the woman he loved whom the ancient Duke had violated, swears to be revenged not only on the Duke, but on his son Lussurio, his bastard Spurio, and the Duchess. From that opening there follows a succession of scenes of horror and death that involves all the characters in the play. Yet Tourneur contrives to give the impression that this is no melodramatic holocaust, but a poetic view of the world, of a cruel, diseased, lecherous, revengeful world, from which there is no escape and in the midst of which there is no pity.

8

John Webster – Beaumont and Fletcher – Philip
Massinger–Thomas Middleton–William Rowley
John Ford – James Shirley

IT IS difficult to mark precisely the division between the drama of Shakespeare and his contemporaries and that of the following age. In Shakespeare himself and in Jonson there is an awareness of a moral world, and a concentration on normality which is less apparent in the later drama. Yet technically and in other ways some of Shakespeare's later plays such as *Cymbeline* differ profoundly from the comedies and histories of the early period. There is a continuous development throughout the first four decades, with, as its most marked feature, an increase in sophistication, and in theatrical as opposed to natural emphasis, while in its later phases there is an exploration of situations and passions that are removed from normality.

While all divisions are thus unsatisfactory, the reader or the audience in the theatre who was familiar only with Shakespeare's work would certainly be aware of a marked change of atmosphere on coming to the plays of John Webster and those of Beaumont and Fletcher. It is with the appearance of their work and that of their successors therefore that a new phase in the drama would appear to begin. John Webster (1575–1625), was a marked contrast to Chapman, for instead of a verbal and reflective complexity which seems untheatrical he shows himself such a master of the stage that his plays whenever adequately presented gain the interest of modern audiences. The whole of Webster's dramatic achievement is difficult to define. He began as a collaborator, but about the year 1612 he produced two tragedies of outstanding individuality and power: *The White Devil* (about 1611–12, published 1612), and *The Duchess of Malfi* (acted before 1614 and published 1623 'as acted privately at Blackfriars and publicly at the Globe'). The two plays have some similarities: they are both based on Italian themes and the events are loosely connected with events which happened in sixteenth-century Italy. Love and revenge are the motives in both plays, and behind them, governing the action and illuminated by the verse, is a world cruel, passionate, irrational, fierce, a view of life which is never far removed from magnificence or corruption.

In *The White Devil*, Brachiano, a duke, falls in love with Vittoria Corombona, wife of Camillo who is nephew of Cardinal Monticelso. The motives of the action lie largely with Vittoria. She has a 'dream' through which she is able to suggest to Brachiano that he shall kill his wife and her husband; and, once conceived, the intrigue is helped by her brother Flamineo, a machiavellian character. The audience is not spared the horrors of these deaths, for Brachiano through a conjuror has an image of the intricate devices by which they are accomplished built up before him. There follows the trial of Vittoria, a scene to which Webster devotes his whole skill. She becomes the centre of the action, and so despite a multiplicity of episodes she remains to the end. She meets tempestuously and with a grand gesture the retribution of the crimes which she initiated. The scene is written with that stormy intensity which characterises so much of Webster's poetry. The Cardinal who should have been her judge becomes her accuser, and she answers him with an undaunted courage. This movement in the play is resolved by Brachiano's rescue of Vittoria, whom he marries. Webster, having exhausted the motives with which his play began, now regroups his characters for a new crisis. Brachiano develops a jealousy of Vittoria, whom he taunts, and she in reply still shows a defiant anger and courage, though it contains elements of retrospective sadness. Thus the play moves to its climax in which revenge and accident so overwhelm the characters that at the close all are killed.

In *The Duchess of Malfi* Webster was using a widely popular story which had been told by Bandello and Belleforest and in English by William Painter. The Duchess, a wealthy widow, secretly marries her steward, Antonio. Her brothers, Ferdinand and the Cardinal, are opposed to any re-marriage. Their motives are confused, for they wish to retain her wealth and they are fearful that she may marry beneath her while Ferdinand has a feeling towards her that, at times, amounts to a sinister passion. The centre of the action lies in Bosola, an evil and melancholic figure, who with a mind corrupt and disappointed sees the whole of life as a thing diseased. He acts as Ferdinand's spy and gives the lovers away. The punishment of the Duchess is contrived with severity and horror. She is tortured and finally strangled and her children are killed. As in the earlier play the ultimate catastrophe overwhelms all the characters including Bosola, who is made to feel a bitter remorse before his death.

The summary of the plots gives no true impression of

Webster's power. In bare narrative they seem baldly melo-dramatic, and improbability competes with violence. But Webster's sombre spirit, aided by his poetic powers, raises them from melodrama to a tragic world. Such is his genius that his characters do not move as in a story, but in this strange, cruel, irrational world which is peculiarly his own. Bosola is the clearest spokesman of that world, for he sees life to be diseased and men and women helpless puppets incapable of steady or reason-able action. This view of life is ultimately philosophical, though Webster supports it with scenes of mechanical horror, such as that of the conjuror in *The White Devil*, or of the dance of the madmen in *The Duchess of Malfi*. Rupert Brooke, in his essay on Webster, emphasises the force and consistency of this vision behind the tragedies: 'Maggots are what the inhabitants of this Universe most suggest and resemble. The sight of their power is only alleviated by the permanent, calm, unfriendly summits and darkness of the background of death and doom. For that is part of Webster's universe. Human beings are writhing grubs in an immense night. And the night is without stars or moon. But it has sometimes a certain quietude in its darkness: but not very much.'

There is in Webster little smooth development of action, little design. He is less interested in the plot as a whole than in the great dramatic scene and he is less occupied by any subtle. presentation of character than in exploiting some moment of great passion. His plays are apt to become a series of theatrically effective crises, bound together by action which at its worst is carelessly contrived. This apparently haphazard development lends a certain brutal force to the plays, as if life itself were governed by chance, not reason, and as if human beings acted from passion rather than from consistent conduct governed by consecutive thought. Yet this will not explain all, for some of the coincidences, improbabilities and forced effects are weaknesses and excesses of dramatic structure and are apparent as such in the theatre.

The moral world of Webster is different from that of Shakespeare. Here love is the sole theme of tragedy, and evil, though it meets retribution, is present everywhere throughout the action. Webster's power lies in the sense of magnificence which accompanies the evil, gaining its supreme illustration in *The White Devil*. Brutal as the world may be, and corrupt as are her motives, Vittoria's audacity and dignity give to her life some great gesture even if it lacks virtue and nobility. In the lyrics which act as it were as a symbol of the mood behind the tragedies Webster seems to suggest the piteousness of life, though he never weakens into sentiment nor relaxes from his vision that violence, corruption and passion are inevitable.

In the later years of Shakespeare's dramatic career there appeared two writers, John Fletcher (1579–1625), and Francis Beaumont (1584–1616), both of great competence, and found frequently working together in happy collaboration. Their clever and sophisticated romantic tragedies and tragi-comedies captured popular taste, and Shakespeare in such a play as *Cymbeline* would seem to have imitated them. Fletcher is the more prolific and the longer lived. His association with Beaumont seems to have begun about 1607 and to have continued to 1616. He also wrote independently, and with Massinger and others. Beaumont died when he was thirty, but he had already combined with Fletcher in a dominating way in a number of plays.

One of the earliest and most successful of their tragi-comedies was *Philaster* (1609–1610). The play has an ingenious plot, newly conceived by the authors, though some of the scenes are reminiscent of scenes in Shakespearian tragedy and comedy. Philaster, the rightful heir to the throne of Sicily, is allowed the freedom of the court by the usurping king. He is loved by this king's daughter, Arethusa, and she is betrothed to Pharamond, a prince of Spain. There are well-contrived scenes early in the play in which Arethusa declares her love for Philaster. The lovers decide to use as a go-between a page, Bellario, who is in fact a girl, Euphrasia. She is in love with Philaster and employs this disguise so that she may be near him. From this basis an elaborate superstructure of misunderstandings and complexities is evolved, all of which are fully exploited. At the conclusion, which is unnatural and complicated, Philaster and Arethusa marry. The play had certain features which remain common to the whole type. So, for instance, the scene was removed from reality and many of its motives were as in romantic comedy, despite the fact that the situations themselves were presented with tragic seriousness. There was little characterisation, but much ingenuity in incident, and many excellent individual scenes, well-contrived theatrically. It is as if error and accident were competing to place the characters in complex and embarrassing situations, as if the world of *Cymbeline*, whose motives belong to romantic comedy, were dignified into tragedy. The characters have no individual strength but exist for the scenes in which they occur, and when at the conclusion they fall outside the overcrowded pattern they are ignored as if they had never existed.

A King and No King (about 1612) followed a similar pattern. The scene was set in Iberia, an unreal country with characters possessing equally unreal names. The theme again is ingenious, invented and unnatural. Arbaces, the king of Iberia, conquers Tigranes, king of Armenia, and offers him noble treatment and his sister for a wife. Tigranes' affections are already committed to Spaconia. Arbaces has not seen his sister Panthea for a long time. When he sees her he is seized with an incestuous passion. Tigranes too, forgetting his own lady, falls in love with Panthea. Arbaces, in anger for this, throws Tigranes into prison, where he repents and is visited by Spaconia, who forgives him. Later it is discovered that Arbaces is the son of the Lord Protector and Panthea is not his sister, so that the way of their love is open. The play has many features which distinguish it from Shakespeare's tragic world. The theme is a dangerous one and handled so as to emphasise its unnatural elements while the tragedy is resolved not by death but by artifice. The characterisation is indistinct, and indeed the interest depends rather on the ingenuity of incident than on the firmness of character portrayal.

In *The Maid's Tragedy* (1610–1611), the authors face a tragic conclusion in a play which retains some of the atmosphere of *Philaster*. It is as if tragi-comedy had been adapted to the revenge play, and it must be admitted that motives are stronger and more natural than in the other plays of this group. The king (of Rhodes this time, but all these are theatrical kingdoms), commands a gentleman, Amintor, to marry Evadne. After the marriage Amintor

D–ED

discovers that Evadne has been mistress to the king. Complex and elaborate action follows, but in the conclusion Evadne kills the king and then takes her own life. Here the whole action is more consistent, at least in its main plot, and the marriage is not such a blatant device as the elements which start the action in the other plays.

It is impossible here to detail the whole activity in drama of Beaumont and Fletcher. Their comic talent, both incidentally in the tragi-comedies and in independent pieces, though dexterous and pleasing to contemporary audiences, is never likely to find its way again to the stage. Two of their plays of very different types are, however, outstanding: *The Knight of the Burning Pestle* (1611, printed 1613), which, though written in collaboration, is mainly Beaumont's work, and *The Faithful Shepherdess* (acted 1608–9), which was Fletcher's brilliant adventure in the poetic, pastoral play.

The Knight of the Burning Pestle owes its origin to the Don Quixote of Cervantes, and is a mock-heroic play, parodying many fashions in the theatre, particularly the 'citizen' plays of Dekker and Heywood. The prologue gives the temper of the acting. A citizen complains that citizens are not depicted respectfully on the stage, and that if Ralph, his apprentice, were given a suit of clothes he could do great deeds. So it is arranged that Ralph shall be a character in the play and the citizen and his wife spectators of the action. Ralph's adventures are in part a parody of the chivalrous romances, and Ralph himself satirises all baseness dressed up in magnificent pseudo-heroic trappings. Apart from this the play is full of memories taken from many sources, including Kyd's *Spanish Tragedy*, while in the plot of Jasper, the apprentice who marries his master's daughter, the values of the romantic plays are effectively satirised.

The Faithful Shepherdess belongs to a very different world. Fletcher makes use of the idealised conventions of the pastoral for a graceful poetic play. The main theme is the love of Amoret, the faithful shepherdess, for Perigot, while the opening motive in which Clorin, a shepherdess, laments her dead love and is tempted by a satyr, is very similar to the theme used later by Milton in *Comus*. Fletcher's verse has very distinct qualities. He uses an eleven-syllable line with frequent feminine endings, that is, endings on an unaccented syllable. A typical example from *The Faithful Shepherdess* is:

'And wanton shepherds be to me delightful.'

This effect is to produce a blank verse less regular than that of many of his predecessors, but very lively. It has a natural effect, and is nearer to conversation than declamation. He can be regular, and at times careless. His language is less compressed than that of Shakespeare, nor does it seem to bear the same pressure of thought. Charles Lamb has described the difference effectively: 'Fletcher lays line upon line, making up one after the other, adding image to image so deliberately that we see where they join. Shakespeare mingles everything: he runs line into line, embraces sentences and metaphors; before one idea has burst its shell another is hatched and clamorous for disclosure.'

Among the dramatists associated with Fletcher was Philip Massinger (1583-1639). He was educated at Oxford and then disappeared into the theatre world of London. His dramatic work suggests that he had a stubborn and independent spirit, and more than once he was in trouble with the authorities for the too candid expression of political views in his plays. In *The Renegado* (about 1624), he made a Catholic a sympathetic and central figure at a time when anti-Catholic spirit was running high. He collaborates with a number of writers, and those who have attempted to isolate his share in these joint contributions discover in his work the continual repetition of the same phrases. With Fletcher he wrote 'humours' comedy, such as *The Little French Lawyer* (about 1619), with a more liberal movement of intrigue than in Jonson. He also wrote with Fletcher *The Spanish Curate* (about 1622), which has lively and ingenious scenes. He emerges into independent work with two powerful comedies which contain elements of Jonsonian 'humours' in them: *A New Way to Pay Old Debts* (by 1626), and *The City Madam* (by 1632). He collaborated again with Fletcher in tragedy, and here the contrast of their natures becomes apparent, for Fletcher is easy, gracious and immoral, while Massinger has probably a religious and certainly a moral outlook. From Fletcher he certainly learned an adroitness in dramatic arrangement but throughout, while he carries a number of reminiscences from other writers, he maintains a great independence of spirit. Among the tragedies in which Massinger combined with Fletcher were *Thierry and Theodoret* (printed 1623), an elaborate but not very effective play on a sixth-century theme; and *The False One*, a play on the love of Caesar and Cleopatra. Massinger wrote other tragedies, some in collaboration and some independently With Dekker he wrote *The Virgin Martyr* (before 1620), a play on the persecution of the Christians under Diocletian. It would seem most probable that the main conception came from Massinger, for he had a strong religious interest. Despite its popularity the tragedy lacks any effectiveness that could give it a permanent hold. It is a horror drama in a Roman setting, and possibly Dekker supplied only the rather poor comic relief. Apart from this work in collaboration Massinger writes three tragedies, which lie between the work of Shakespeare and Webster and the more decadent school of Tourneur, Ford and Shirley. In *The Unnatural Combat* (1623) he employs the themes of parricide and incest in a free treatment of the Cenci story. In *The Duke of Milan* (printed 1623) the death of one of the characters is contrived by the fact that the face of a dead woman had poison placed on it. The most impressive of these tragedies is *The Roman Actor* (1626). The play is set in the reign of Domitian and the main character is the actor Paris. Here, while there is horror and an atmosphere of decadence, one is aware also of elements not present in the other plays. Above all there is Paris's conception of the art of the actor and his plea for the theatre. The final movement depends on the murder of Paris by Domitian.

The two comedies in which Massinger's genius is most distinctly revealed are serious in intent. He employs 'humours' comedy for a moral purpose. Little is known of Massinger's relations with Jonson. It has been surmised that they were unfriendly, but whatever may have been their personal feelings Massinger obviously studied Jonson's comedy closely. *A New Way to Pay Old Debts* (published 1623) has had a very long and successful history on the stage. This is a tribute to its well-constructed plot and the strong but simple lines of its characterisation. The main 'humours' figure is Sir Giles Overreach, and his cruelty and callousness are clearly etched out and emphasised in the play. The plot of the play is the 'untrussing' of Overreach, who is outmanoeuvred in his project of effecting a wealthy but unromantic marriage for his daughter Margaret. She helps in the process and gains the young man whom she wants, Tom Allworth. Overreach is the strongest dramatic portraiture in the play, and he represents something which Massinger was often trying to reveal; for he has the unscrupulous and evil cruelty which parallels that of Domitian in *The Roman Actor*.

The City Madam (1632) is a much later play, but it has the same atmosphere of confident competence. On this occasion it is a woman whom Massinger satirises in the person of Lady Frugal. In both the plays the characters are of a citizen type. The whole setting is removed from the courtly background of Fletcher's plays and the values are different. The citizens are not comically portrayed, but their loves and emotions are explored seriously and often in a mood of satire. *The City Madam* is, in some ways, a transition from the 'humours' play of Jonson to the 'manners' comedy of Congreve. Lady Frugal is a proud, extravagant female martinet, who rules her daughters and her husband's raffish brother. The moral is expressed in the conclusion by Sir John Frugal:

> Make you good
> Your promised reformation, and instruct
> Our city dames, whom wealth makes proud, to move
> In their own spheres; and willingly to confess
> In their habits, manners, and their highest port
> A distance 'twixt the city and the court.

One of the best scenes is that in which Lady Frugal tries
to make an astrologer show the suitors for her daughters'
hands how they should use them. The scene is very like
the courtship of Millamant and Mirabell in Congreve's
The Way of the World.

The career of Thomas Middleton (1580–1627),
stretches over a long period of the drama. His biography,
like that of most dramatists of the period, remains
obscure. Born in 1580, and not as was previously con-
jectured in 1570, he was educated at Oxford and by 1602
there are already payments entered for him in Henslowe's
diary as part-author of plays. He attempted both comedy
and tragedy, and he worked both alone and in collaboration. Much of his early work lay in comedy. Miss Ellis-
Fermor has noted in the early comedies an easy accept-
ance of life similar to that found in Chaucer, and Middleton himself referred to Chaucer as 'that broad, famous
English poet'. Such is the atmosphere of *A Trick to Catch
the Old One* (published 1608), where a setting in citizen
life allows of many amusing devices and of an atmosphere
which is good-humoured if moral values are not questioned too closely. A change comes with *A Chaste Maid
of Cheapside* (about 1613), where a far more sardonic
mood prevails and satire has replaced gaiety. The
main plot reveals how the parents of the chaste girl, Moll,
plot to force her into marriage with a dissolute Welsh
knight, Sir Walter Whorehound. This change of mood,
which leads ultimately to tragi-comedy and tragedy, may
possibly have been due to the influence of William
Rowley. Middleton was also the author of *The Witch*, a
play not successful at the time and preserved in
manuscript until 1778. The figure of Hecate and the

witches' songs were transcribed from this into the corrupt Folio text of *Macbeth*.

Of William Rowley little is known except that he was an actor and that he collaborated with Middleton. After two less successful attempts in *A Fair Quarrel* (published 1617) and *The Spanish Gipsy* (performed before Prince Charles in Whitehall, 1623), the two authors contrived together a memorable play in *The Changeling* (1623, published 1653). The title is derived from a negligible comic underplot which may be Rowley's work. The main plot is built up with great dramatic skill and touches the emotions deeply. The audience is thrown, almost violently, into the midst of the action. Alsemero loves Beatrice, who is bethrothed to Piracquo. De Flores, the evil genius of the tragedy, loves Beatrice, but she hates him. To save herself from her own dilemma Beatrice lays herself in De Flores' power by consenting that he shall kill Piracquo. Gradually Beatrice comes to realise that the price De Flores intends to extract for his action is her love. The scenes between them are handled with great power:

> Why 'tis impossible thou canst be so wicked,
> Or shelter such a cunning cruelty,
> To make his death the murderer of my honour!
> Thy language is so bold and vicious
> I cannot see which way I can forgive it
> With any modesty.

To which De Flores replies:

> Pish! you forget yourself
> A woman dipped in blood, and talk of modesty.

The conclusion is presented with sustained force. Beatrice's evil deed is discovered by Alsemero and she suffers death at the hands of De Flores who then kills himself. In some strange way the audience is made to realise that these figures are more than puppets. They have an individual strength despite their evil, for De Flores has consistency and Beatrice a romantic devotion which transcends all moral values. The verse has poignancy and the whole is so well contrived that the tragedy stands high amid those of the period.

It was probably before *The Changeling* that Middleton had written independently the tragedy of *Women Beware Women* (about 1620), a play of involved sexual intrigue. As one of its motives he used a game of chess played by two of the characters. To this theme of chess he returned with great skill in a satiric play with a political theme, *A Game at Chess* (acted 1624). The play is based on the proposals of a Spanish marriage for Prince Charles which was planned by Gondomar, the Spanish Ambassador. The whole project was unpopular with the public, and when the Prince returned from Madrid without the bride there was great popular rejoicing. Middleton's play answered this feeling and had great success until the Spanish Ambassador intervened.

Outstanding among the later Stuart dramatists was John Ford (1586–1604). He had commenced a career as a writer as early as 1606 with an elegiac poem, but his work for the stage comes later. The best of it is to be found in *The Witch of Edmonton*, where he collaborated with Rowley and Dekker; *The Lovers' Melancholy* (acted 1628, published 1629); *Love's Sacrifice* (published 1633); *The Broken Heart* (published 1633); and *'Tis Pity She's a Whore* (published 1633). *The Broken Heart* illustrates Ford's power in tragedy. The play is one of horror with the elevation of passion and its inevitability as a substitute for a moral motive. It is the same sense of romantic destiny which is urged to justify the sensuous love of Giovanni for his sister Annabella in *'Tis Pity She's a Whore*. In *'Tis Pity* the verse has gravity and argument, but the scenes are spectacles of horror, curiously contrived. They culminate in a scene where Giovanni, having killed Annabella, rushes in among the guests with her heart at the end of his sword.

James Shirley (1596–1666), has claims to be considered the last of the dramatists of the Elizabethan and Stuart periods. His career as a dramatist extends from 1625 to the closing of the theatres in 1642. He was on the king's side in the Civil War, and after the Restoration he returned to London where his plays were still popular, though he did not add to their number. He lost his house in the Great Fire of 1666, and soon after both he and his wife died on the same day. A large number of his plays survive, for when the Puritans closed the theatres Shirley turned his attention from the production of plays to the printing of them. He ranges from comedy and tragicomedy to tragedy. Shirley himself thought that his tragedy, *The Cardinal* (1641), was the best of his plays. It is an honest opinion, though some think he overestimated the strength of this, the last of his tragedies. Already ten years previously, in *The Traitor* (1631, printed 1635), he had written a play of equal power. *The Traitor* is a free treatment of the career of Lorenzo de Medici. It is a brilliant and macabre picture of the ambitious and licentious duke, who worked his way through a mass of intrigue in order to gain his own passionate end. Finally he oversteps himself and is overwhelmed in a scene of massed horrors. F. S. Boas, in an excellent summary of this play, suggests that as 'the test of tragic art does not lie in the number of victims at the close', the play, 'hovering often between rhetoric and poetry' misses true greatness.

The Cardinal owes much to Webster, but to a Webster who has been fairly and purposefully studied. The Cardinal himself is the central interest of the play, though he is held in the background until the fifth act. At first he seems merely a schemer anxious to help his nephew to marry Rosaura. She instead marries D'Alvarez, and at the wedding festivities the nephew and other masquers enter and lead D'Alvarez away with them and then bring back his corpse and throw it at her feet. In all this the Cardinal has seemed but a subsidiary figure, but he now comes forward to a horrible and dominating prominence. Ultimately he kills Rosaura and meets his own death. The play is wholly involved in horror, and it is with horror that there ends the great series of plays which had begun in Elizabethan times over half a century earlier.

In 1642 the theatres were closed by an ordinance which affirmed that 'public sports do not well agree with public calamities, nor public stage-plays with the seasons of humiliation'. There were, however, some private performances, and plays were still published even when they could not be performed. The main link between the pre-war period and the Restoration was Sir William Davenant (1606–68), son of a vintner of Oxford, and some would say Shakespeare's godson. His father was a man of substance and William himself chose the road to the court and not to the university and became page to the Duchess of Richmond. Of his life in the years which follow more is known than of many of his contemporaries. He had a link with the older Elizabethan age by his service with Sir Fulke Greville, Sir Philip Sidney's friend, and his contact with King Charles was shown by his appointment in 1633 to the Laureateship in succession to Ben Jonson. In between he had killed his man in a duel and had gained pardon for the homicide after a threat of transportation. He was later involved in royalist plots and in 1642 he was on the Continent with the king's court. One of his later adventures led him back to England and to imprisonment but, with luck of which he seems to have had a generous share, he gained a pardon from Cromwell. Throughout the whole of this strange and varied career he retained a strong ambition to succeed as a dramatist. From 1656 he was already organising entertainments in 'private places' with the help of a few highly-placed Puritan sympathisers. In 1656 he contrived to produce *The Siege of Rhodes*, an entertainment in verse with music, and thus, through a form of opera, drama came back to the stage. In 1658 he also produced two similar pieces, *The Cruelty of the Spaniards in Peru*, and *The History of Francis Drake*. Neither has any notable dramatic merit, but they are evidence of Davenant's determination to keep the drama alive despite all difficulties. In May, 1660, Charles II was recalled, and the necessity of all subterfuge as far as the performance of drama was concerned had passed.

9

The Restoration Period

THE theatre of the years 1660–1700 differed profoundly from that of the days of the Elizabethan age and of the early seventeenth century. In the early period the dramatist still had a sense of community with the whole of society. It is true that one eye might be kept firmly on the court, but his heart and sensibilities extended to very many sections of the people. There is no *A Midsummer Night's Dream* in the Restoration period. Something died out of England with the Civil War and the sense of loss, profound, though most often intangible, can be felt in the drama. The theatre was more closely than ever the province of the Court, and the audiences consisted largely of the courtiers and their entourage. The mind of England in these last forty years of the seventeenth century does not come out fully in the drama, for the work of the Royal Society, of Bunyan and of Locke belongs to these years, sober and steady work which has no reflection in the traffic of the stage. Yet, as fortunately can be recorded through the notes of an intelligent playgoer such as Samuel Pepys, the taste of the age extended beyond the new and fashionable plays of its own production to an enjoyment of Shakespeare, Ben Jonson, and many other earlier writers.

Narrow though the new talents of the Restoration period may have been, they were elegant and distinguished. At the centre of all lies John Dryden (1631–

1700), with his varied achievement in comedy, heroic play and tragedy, and above all his critical capacity for estimating his own and other men's literary attainments. The drama has to wait for the days of G. B. Shaw before once again a practising dramatist writes in such an illuminating way about his art. From all the varied work that the age produces two types seem most representative. Heroic tragedy seems to symbolise the longing of the age for an idealism which it can never practise, an apotheosis of love and honour by audiences and dramatists who have come to regard the honest expression of both as impossible. On the other hand lies the comedy of manners, cynical, elegant and witty, almost as if it were the amoral realism of courtly life. There is this difference between the two types, that while heroic tragedy pleased its own age and has pleased no other, being indeed at its worst some pathology of drama, the comedy of manners has rightly found a permanent place in the repertory of the English stage, wherever there are audiences not dominated by squeamishness in theatrical taste.

The earliest of the writers to practise the comedy of manners was Sir George Etherege (1635–1691). He is remembered for three comedies: *The Comical Revenge* (1664); *She Would If She Could* (1668); and *The Man of Mode* (1676). Etherege was the first who realised that comedy in the manner of Molière could be exploited in English, and while he has little of Molière's skill and none of his delicacy his work proved very popular. So successful was his second play that when Mr. Pepys went to see it he could find no room in the pit and had, grudgingly, to pay for a box. *The Man of Mode*, typical of his plays, has very little story or plot. There is love intrigue, but as everyone is engaged in that all the time it seems a routine rather than part of a plot. The hero is Dorimont, a fashionable character who can turn the temper of a woman with an epigram and excuse his own conduct with a paradox. In his love intrigues he exploits the foolishness of Sir Fopling Flutter, a pseudo-courtier full of French fashions.

Etherege's success led naturally to a number of imitations such as Sir Charles Sedley's *The Mulberry Garden* (1668), which followed the general pattern of Etherege's *The Comical Revenge* while borrowing certain details from Molière. A far more powerful mind entered into the comedy of manners in William Wycherley (1640–1716). His reputation is based upon four plays: *Love in a Wood* (1671); *The Gentleman Dancing-Master* (1672); *The Country Wife* (1675); and *The Plain Dealer* (1676). The earliest play, *Love in a Wood*, deals with contemporary fashionable life and, following Sedley's *The Mulberry Garden*, has its setting in St. James' Park, a scene which would be recognised by all the audience. The plot consists of love intrigues which are sufficiently complicated and numerous to rob the play of its unity and design. The plot of *The Gentleman Dancing-Master*, which has some broadly farcical elements, turns on the device of the heroine who attempts to hide her lover by pretending that he is a dancing-master. The play has some satiric comment on the manners of the age, and there are characters in whom Spanish and French manners are parodied. *The Country Wife* has a stronger plot, even if it is a more unpleasant play. The debt to Molière is considerable, yet despite these derivations the spirit and much of the conduct of the play are original. The tone is coarse in the extreme, but behind the lewdness one has the impression of a strong, sardonic mind. One feels that one is in the presence of the satirist of Restoration comedy though an incomplete satirist. The satirist should be one who does not accept the values of the society which he condemns. Wycherley's motives are not so integrated. It is contempt rather than moral condemnation which he expresses. Most often one feels that there is a sardonic mind which knows all that is most obscene in his age. and contrives somehow to despise it and indulge in it simultaneously.

The Plain Dealer was the last and most effective of Wycherley's plays, and in this he shows that he was aware of the criticisms that had been made against the obscenities of *The Country Wife*. The play owes much to Molière's *Le Misanthrope*, though Wycherley's individual spirit still remains. The central character is Manly, the Alceste of Molière's play: 'an unmannerly sea-dog', he shows a hatred for all men and yet conceals a very definite love beneath the hatred. Wycherley has given his play a much fuller movement of intrigue and incident than Molière found it necessary to employ. While Molière concentrates on Alceste, Wycherley adds to the story of Manly a varied and interesting movement of comic life. Wycherley was condemned by Macaulay for depriving Molière's play of its strength and beauty; but Wycherley had to adapt the figure of Alceste in the person of Manly to the condition of contemporary English society. A sympathetic French critic, Perromat, has realised this: 'If Manly had spoken the language of Alceste the picture of the century would not be real and the public would not recognise it'. Wycherley is affected by the native influence

of Jonson, as well as by Molière, and some of the character-
istics of Manly seem to arise from a 'humours' conception.

William Congreve (1670–1729), was the last and greatest of Restoration writers of comedy. Suddenly at the
age of twenty-five he achieved fame with *The Old Bachelor*
(1693). Only three comedies followed: *The Double Dealer*
(1693); *Love for Love* (1695); and *The Way of the World*
(1700). In the middle of these he wrote a tragedy, *The
Mourning Bride* (1697). At the age of thirty his career as a
dramatist was over. There is very little true comedy in
English and in that small circle Congreve is supreme. For
comedy is more than farce, the play where untoward
incidents render the characters ridiculous, and it is also
more than the play of intrigue with a happy ending,
which the histories of drama so often for convenience
classify under comedy. Nor is it burlesque, for there the
movement, however amusing, depends upon some life
other than its own. Comedy, in its truest interpretation,
depends, as Meredith saw, upon a conception of society,
and the comic writer will hold up the mirror to his age,
depicting its eccentricities, its deviations from some
agreed norm. The society and the audience must be aware
of the 'finer shades'. If the society is moral the comedy
will reveal the variations from a moral norm, but in
Restoration comedy the errors are not those of a moral
code but of deviations from wit and good manners. For
such a comedy Congreve could draw on Ben Jonson and
Molière. Ben Jonson, though he knew what comedy
should be, never found the society with the 'finer shades',
though he approaches it in *The Alchemist* and in parts of
The Silent Woman. Molière lived in a different world, one
of gentility, with its own elaborate and gracious con-
ED–E

ventions. A man might be commendable morally and yet fail in that world. He must conduct himself so that he is acceptable to society. This inevitable relation of comedy to society explains the licence of Restoration comedy, for if there was to be a comedy at all based on that society it had to be licentious. The theatre was full of members of the court and of the looser elements amid the gentry, and the gallery of footmen and servants, and the women wore masks. They all knew what to expect. Charles Lamb, the great apologist of Restoration drama, defends it as artificial and fanciful and therefore harmless. Macaulay rebuked him in a heavy-handed way, but he was right at least to this extent that he saw how this comedy was based on a conception of a real and contemporary society.

Congreve, unlike Shakespeare, built only one world in his plays, and the same values hold for all his comedies. A character could walk from one play to another and still find himself at home. There is a systematic conception behind that world. Tragedy and pathos must not enter in, and the display of emotion is rather bad taste. Elegance and wit are essential, and morality is tedious, and above all one must not speak from the heart. Much that has been written of Congreve is unhappy and untrue, and some critics, including Thackeray who should have known better, have indulged in mere vituperation. Some of the best things have been written by Swinburne: 'Congreve's intellect is clear, cold, and narrow; it has the force and brightness of steel; the edges of it, so to speak, are cut out hard and sharp. There is more weight and matter in Congreve than in any English dramatist since the Restoration; and at worst he is no coarser than his time. In Congreve all is plain and clear if hard and limited; he makes no effort to escape into the region of moral sentiment; if his world is not healthy neither is it hollow; and whatever he had of noble humour and feeling was genuine and genial. His style is a model of grace and accurate vigour, and his verbal wit the most brilliant and forcible in English literature. We do not say that it was pure and exalted; such properties belong to other times and other minds. But as a comic writer he stands above the best who came after him and beside the best who went before.'

The Old Bachelor already shows something of Congreve's skill, though the action is excessively encumbered with intrigue. The title theme is the adventure of Heartwell, the old bachelor, who is nearly decoyed into marriage. Here, as often in Restoration comedy, there are two groups of characters, the 'wits' who claim our sympathy and the 'gulls', the dull ones. The conclusion is not a triumph of good over evil, but of the keen over the stupid. Both sides may be equally bad, but that does not count in the play. The 'wits', whatever they may lack, do at least possess grace and style. They are never nonplussed and retain a certain attractiveness whatever they may do.

Possibly Congreve was told by his friends that the plot of *The Old Bachelor* was weak, for in *The Double Dealer* he was thinking about plot and about the theory of drama. The plot becomes clear, but too important for a comedy of manners. In compensation *Love for Love* is one of the best comedies of manners in the language, and the enduring quality of its appeal was shown in the great success of its revival during the years of the

Second World War. It is clear that there is one dominant intrigue and that all the others branch from it. Sir Sampson promises to pay the debts of his son Valentine if he will allow the inheritance to go to Ben, a younger sailor son. Ben refuses the match that Sir Sampson proposes, and so the old man thinks of marriage himself. His eye falls on Angelica, who is in love with Valentine but has not declared her love. She falls in with Sir Sampson's wishes far enough to free Valentine from the stern plans of his father. There are excellent and well-disciplined subsidiary actions with clearly contrived characters such as Mrs. Foresight and Mrs. Frail. The opening is inimitable, and throughout Congreve is in the happy exercise of all his powers. The audience is carried into the midst of the action on a stream of witty thought.

There followed in 1700 *The Way of the World*, the most elaborate and in some ways the most brilliant of Congreve's comedies. The plot is complicated and improbable, and misses the virtues of simple directness which *Love for Love* possessed. Congreve meditated long on the plot, and perhaps he meditated too long. He rids himself of such devices as the aside and the soliloquy which he had used so freely in *The Double Dealer*, but in doing so he leaves the movement of the action a little obscure. Much of the first act is occupied with the presentation of plot, particularly the theme of Mirabell's love for Millamant, the niece of Lady Wishfort. Millamant is to lose half her fortune if she marries without Lady Wishfort's consent. It is only when this tediousness with the mechanism of the action is over that Millamant, perhaps the most brilliant woman in English comedy, is allowed to appear. The scenes between her and Mirabell are the most excellent in the whole of the comedy of that age. The characterisation has a subtlety which separates it from any obvious portrayal of type and gives to this play a delicacy all its own.

In 1697 Congreve published his one tragedy: *The Mourning Bride*. This should properly be considered with the other tragedies of the age, with Otway and Rowe, though something may be gained by placing it here with the rest of Congreve's work. It is a good stage play, as one would expect from Congreve. To some extent it has been under-estimated, probably as a reaction against Samuel Johnson's extravagant praise in his life of Congreve. The play was very popular and held the stage in the eighteenth century. The weakness lies in the inadequacy of the characters, and one is left with a story of romantic incident dramatized, full of mystery and surprises, but lacking a powerful fable from which a true tragic crisis could emerge.

The vogue of the comedy of manners was partly affected by the attack in 1698 by Jeremy Collier, entitled *Short View of the Profaneness and Immorality of the English Stage*. This led to a pamphlet warfare, and it was clear that however clumsily he conducted his argument there was something to be said on Collier's side. Further, his publication coincided with the beginning of a change in public taste. The manners comedy did not, however, disappear completely, for in the early years of the new century it was broadened and humanised by two competent practitioners, George Farquhar (1678–1707) and Sir John Vanbrugh (1664–1726). Farquhar began with two comedies of no particular distinction, *Love in a Bottle* (1699) and *A Constant Couple* (1699). These he followed by two far more interesting and mature comedies, *The Recruiting Officer* (1706) and *The Beaux Stratagem* (1707). He has a wider movement of life than Congreve, so the recruiting scene in *The Recruiting Officer* and the opening of *The Beaux Stratagem* in an inn at Lichfield have a realistic interest such as is found in the eighteenth-century periodical essays and the novel.

Other elements also separate these plays from Congreve and give them a pleasing individuality. *The Recruiting Officer* occupies itself in part with the methods of recruiting. This may have a theatrical ancestry in Falstaff, but Farquhar is not relying on that source. He is satirising the recruiting methods of his own time. In the scene before the Justices he employs a number of contemporary details, and these, with the satire, add to the realism of the play. Yet, while introducing these new features, he is faithful, in the main mood, to the manners type of comedy. He lacks the brilliance in dialogue of Congreve, though he shares his general immoral tone. He uses farce more freely, and he has a little of the sentimentality which was later to become dominant in the drama. The main plot is of how Silvia, a young heiress, dressed up as a soldier and strutted out impertinently and spoke as grossly as any trooper, so that she might marry Captain Plume of whom her father disapproved. The sentimental element appears when, suddenly and with some incongruity, Silvia makes a serious speech on marriage and the position of women. *The Beaux Stratagem*, a delightful play, which has always been given a welcome when it is competently revived, shares a number of features with *The Recruiting Officer*. The main plot still has much of the quality of a manners play, but it is acted out with a greater variety of adventure. Two gentlemen with depleted fortunes, Aimwell and Archer, arrive at Lichfield. Aimwell gains the love of a charming and clever young lady, who is married to a sottish country squire named Sullen. There is a movement of farce in the plot, mainly supplied by Scrub, the servant of the Sullens, but there is also a serious criticism of the hardship of marriage for women, when economic interests and not affection control. The difference of mood can be seen by a comparison of the discussion of marriage in the fifth act of this play with the witty, premarriage discussion of Millamant and Mirabell in *The Way of the World.* Farquhar has less wit, but the sentiment which Congreve excludes is here given a right of entry and leads to serious discussion. At the same time it would be erroneous to think that the whole play dwells in this atmosphere.

Sir John Vanbrugh is a remarkable personality whose range of achievement cannot easily be estimated as it does not lie within the limits of any one art. His greatest contribution was perhaps as an architect, for he was the designer of Castle Howard, his own Haymarket Theatre, Blenheim Palace and other great projects. He wrote a number of comedies of which the soundest is probably *The Provok'd Wife* (1697), as *The Confederacy* (1705), is the most immoral. The main plot of *The Provok'd Wife* turns upon the matrimonial cruelty of Sir John Brute, and on his wife's cynical attitude to virtue and faithfulness. The main movement of the play still arises from the same world as manners comedy, though a far more liberal use is made of farcical elements. The wit of Congreve is absent, but there is some compensation in the satirical attitude which is well maintained. It is found particularly in the portrait of Sir John Brute, a character who seems to look back to the 'humours' types of Jonson, and even of Massinger in *A New Way to Pay Old Debts*.

While comedy thus flourished in the Restoration period, a number of more serious types of drama also maintained their popularity. There remained throughout a strong affection for the tragi-comedies of Beaumont and Fletcher. The other Elizabethans, including Shakespeare, were often performed, though sometimes in remodelled or amended versions. Davenant's *Siege of Rhodes* (1656) had introduced a taste for musical entertainment. This was enhanced by the introduction, with the turn of the century, of Italian operas of the regular type, though the innovation was not achieved without opposition. Among the attempts to compose opera in the Italian manner in English was Addison's *Rosamond* of 1707. This was accounted a failure, but later some regular imitations from the Italian were better received. The only outstanding British success in the eighteenth century was to come with John Gay's satirical ballad opera, *The Beggar's Opera* (1728), which he followed with *Polly* in 1729.

The strangest and most distinctive type of play that developed was the 'heroic tragedy' to which a brief reference has already been made. This type of drama certainly answered some desire in the audience to see love and honour treated in a grand manner on an unreal scene. No one will ever revive these plays on the stage, and their importance would be small had not such a powerful mind as that of Dryden occupied itself so closely with their composition and their criticism. Much that is most interesting in Dryden's essays is concerned with heroic tragedy. For Dryden the 'Heroic Play' is tragedy: it must have a noble theme, and noble expression, by which he means the heroic couplet. Ideally the play should be regularly constructed with a single theme, and if possible with the preservation of the unities. In fact, as Dryden says in *An Essay on Heroic Plays*, 'an heroic play ought to be an imitation in little of the heroic poem'. For the actual origin of the species Dryden would give some credit to Davenant's *The Siege of Rhodes*, in its later version as a play, though he admitted that it lacked strength and characterisation. He quotes boldly from Ariosto as his other inspiration, and states that love and valour and honour must be the motives of the action. Another influence was certainly the French prose romances which were so popular in England in the late seventeenth century.

Roger Boyle, Earl of Orrery (1621–1679), attempted heroic tragedy in unhistorical English history in *Henry V* (1664), and *The Black Prince* (1667); and at the same time Dryden with Sir Robert Howard produced *The Indian Queen* (1664). The theme is of Montezuma, the conqueror of the Mexicans, just at his moment of triumph, and the action is in a very fanciful setting based on heroic love. The play was successful and was immediately followed with *The Indian Emperor* (1665). Then in 1670 came the most expansive and fanciful of all the heroic plays, *The Conquest of Granada by the Spaniards* in ten acts. It was here that Dryden seems confident that heroic tragedy is the best of all forms of drama produced in the most learned and elegant of all ages:

> If *Love* and *Honour* now are higher rais'd,
> 'Tis not the poet, but the age is prais'd.

> Wits now arriv'd to a more high degree
> Our native language more refin'd and free.

He affirmed that the conception of his hero, Almanzor, was based on the Achilles of Homer and on Tasso's Rinaldo, while some of the incidents were derived from the French heroical romances. Almanzor is the perfectly chivalrous warrior who maintains himself in the world of high honour with an unending supply of rhetoric, written in high-sounding couplets.

In 1675 Dryden composed *Aureng-Zebe*, the most sober and the last of his contributions to this type. The scene is set in India, the India of heroic drama. The play shows the nobleness of Aureng-Zebe as he struggles against the faithlessness of his father, his brothers, and indeed of all around him.

It is clear from the prefatory verses to *Aureng-Zebe* that Dryden was growing tired of the composition of these grandiose heroic tragedies in rhymed verse. There was further in the 'seventies a change of taste that led back towards the more varied and real world of Shakespearian and Stuart tragedy. That Dryden himself had deeply admired this earlier tragedy appears almost everywhere in his critical work. It is true that his affection was tempered sometimes with a belief that they were 'giants before the flood', not fully aware of the elegance and refinements that a more modern age had introduced. Now in 1677 he returned to blank verse, and in *All For Love* wrote a play on the Antony and Cleopatra theme. He indulges in no slavish imitation of Shakespeare's play, though the composition shows again Dryden's admiration for Shakespeare. It is a play arising from a common source in Plutarch, with Shakespeare's tragedy employed at will but with judgement. Dryden breaks down the widely distributed scenes of Shakespeare and brings the theme as close to the unity of action as its nature will permit. The picture of Antony is less generous than in Shakespeare, for the emphasis is on the very last phase, full of fretting and nerves and morbid suspicion. Nor has Cleopatra the 'infinite variety' that she once possessed. *Antony and Cleopatra* was the play in which Shakespeare approached the values of the Restoration stage most closely, for this is the only one of his mature tragedies in which love is made the dominant theme. *All For Love*, of all Dryden's plays, is the one in which the Restoration motives of love and honour are subordinated, and their place taken by suspicion and jealousy.

Dryden was not alone in returning to a more Elizabethan manner in the 'seventies for Thomas Otway and Nathaniel Lee adventured into the same field, and later, in the eighteenth century, they were followed by Nicholas Rowe. Of these the most distinctive was Thomas Otway (1652–85). He had begun with rhymed tragedies, following without any distinguishing excellence the fashion of the age in *Alcibiades* (1674) and *Don Carlos* (1676). He turned to blank verse with *The History and Fall of Caius Marius* (1679). This deals superficially with the quarrel of Marius and Sulla, but its main movement is an adaptation of *Romeo and Juliet* to a Roman setting. Previously *Romeo and Juliet*, 'revised' and played as a tragi-comedy, had not been a popular play on the Restoration stage. Pepys in 1662 had described it as 'the worst that ever I heard in my life'. Much of the attraction of Otway's version lay in the comic parts, particularly that of the Nurse which was played by a man. Its interest lay in

Otway's return, by a route however devious, from the conventional drama popular in his day, to Shakespeare. He followed this pastiche with two original blank verse dramas which are outstanding in the period, *The Orphan* (1680), and *Venice Preserv'd* (1682).

The Orphan is a tragedy of two brothers, Castalio and Polydore, who both love Monimia. She plans to marry Castalio secretly, but Polydore overhears this and thinking their love illicit plans to take Castalio's place. As a result of this action all the characters are overwhelmed by disaster. The weakness of the play lies in its characterisation, for it is unexplained why Polydore should act so brutally, or why, given the relation of the brothers, Castalio should remain so silent about his marriage. In compensation there is the strength of the pathos with which Monimia's position is portrayed. The play had sufficient appeal, particularly in its emotional scenes, to be for a long time a popular revival on the stage. *Venice Preserv'd* has a firmer dramatic basis. The play centres around the character of Jaffeir who is led by debt into a conspiracy with Pierre and others against the State. He is drawn as a vacillating character and is led, first to swear his allegiance to the conspirators, and then by the influence of Belvidera, the woman he loves, to betray them. After the capture of Pierre, Jaffeir feels a second remorse, and, as Pierre is on the scaffold, Jaffeir first kills him and then stabs himself to death. In the final scene the ghost of Pierre appears to Belvidera and she dies. The story may seem melodramatic and ineffective, but it has a strong theatrical quality, and again Otway is able to concentrate on emotion and the portrayal of pathos. It was in pathos also that Nicholas Rowe (1674–

1718), gained his most notable effects in the early eighteenth century with *The Fair Penitent* (1703), *The Tragedy of Jane Shore* (1714), and *The Tragedy of Lady Jane Grey* (1715).

Such were some of the main types of drama that flourished in the Restoration period. Among more miscellaneous pieces, an historical interest at least attaches to Buckingham's burlesque play of *The Rehearsal* (1671). The work may have been by a number of hands, but the main author was the Earl of Buckingham (1625–87), whom Dryden later satirised as Zimri. The features of contemporary drama here satirised and burlesqued are numerous. The central motive is the criticism of the heroic plays, and this appears mainly in the love of Chloris and Prince Prettyman, while a number of lines and couplets from plays of this type are parodied. Together with this there is a personal attack on Dryden who is accused of immorality, vanity and stupidity. Of other writers for the stage Thomas Shadwell (1640–92), can probably never escape from Dryden's brilliant satire of him in *MacFlecknoe*. If with modest talents one is to carry an unsullied reputation into posterity it is obviously wiser not to quarrel and incense such a master of verbal venom as Dryden. Later critics have found much to say in his defence and to discover virtues in *The Sullen Lovers* (1668), and *Epsom Wells* (1672). He continued in a rather heavy-handed way with 'humours' comedy long after the vogue for it had passed. Mrs. Aphra Behn (1640–1689), deserves some notice as the first professional dramatist who was a woman. She had an adventurous career and was obviously endowed with intelligence and determination. She rescued herself from a debtor's prison by relying on her pen, and beginning with tragi-comedy in *The Forc'd Marriage* (1670), she developed with some success into a comedy of intrigue such as *The Rover* (1677 and second part 1680). Her plays have liveliness but they are neither as interesting nor as vivacious as her own life.

The theatre itself in its physical conditions had changed considerably in the Restoration period. The King had ordained that in London there should be only two licensed theatrical ventures. In 1682 they joined into a single monopoly and so remained until 1695. This concentration of all regular dramatic talent and activity into a very limited number of theatres resulted in an inevitable submission of the drama to the Court, and this accounts for many features of the theatrical taste of the period. Further, the Restoration stage developed elaborate scenery, and with the abandonment of the old Elizabethan apron-stage an approach was made to the modern picture-frame setting for a play. The standard of acting was high and the male players were now strengthened by women actresses for the female roles. The King ordained it, and those of his subjects who attended the theatre approved it. So in a period of strange and unequal vigour the courtly drama of the Restoration came to an end with the passing of the Stuart Kings.

I O

The Eighteenth Century

IT CANNOT be denied that the eighteenth century and the first fifty years of the nineteenth were, with the exception of only some half-a-dozen names, a dreary period as far as dramatic authorship is concerned. Recently the whole of this vast and seldom elevated tract of drama has been explored in detail and with the accumulation of much fresh information by Professor Allardyce Nicoll, and anyone coming after him must acknowledge a debt. For he has orderliness and patience in making a reasonable chronicle of years when dullness often reigns in unchallenged supremacy over the theatre.

A number of reasons may be advanced for this declension. The physical conditions of the theatre itself were unfavourable. In the Restoration period London, by which must be understood the Court and its adherents, were content as has been seen with a very limited number of theatres. In the early eighteenth century several little theatres developed, and in these some excellent performances were given. Then in 1737 the Licensing Act cut at the very heart of drama and all regular dramatic presentations were confined to Drury Lane and Covent Garden. Such were the conditions which prevailed until the act of 1843 made the opening of new theatres possible. The audience widened in the early eighteenth century and the citizen or middle-class elements were no longer tolerant of the moral laxity of the Restoration audiences. At the same time it must be confessed that these earlier audiences had taste and discernment and a dread of dullness which the middle-class patrons of drama in the eighteenth century most notably lacked.

There developed in contrast to the hard cynicism of manners comedy a drama of sensibility in which pathos and delicacy and refined sentiments found a place. Colley Cibber, for instance, in such a play as *The Careless Husband* (1704), while he retained much that belonged to the manners tradition, superimposed moral and didactic elements. More important than Cibber was Sir Richard Steele (1672–1729), who wrote a number of plays of sensibility: *The Funeral* (1701): *The Lying Lover* (1703); *The Tender Husband* (1705), and *The Conscious Lovers* (1722). *The Funeral* has a number of manners elements with moralising as a sort of addendum. In *The Lying Lover* he sets his aim with greater precision: 'to banish out of Conversation all Entertainment which does not proceed from Simplicity of Mind, Good-Nature, Friendship and Honour'. Despite these declarations and motives, a number of the moods of manners comedy are retained, though their direction is modified finally to an edifying conclusion. In *The Tender Husband* the sensibility motive was more completely fused into the play as a whole. The conception of *The Conscious Lovers* is based on Terence's *Andria*, but the plot is transformed beyond recognition in the cause of sentimentalism, and at the conclusion of the second act Steele abandons his Latin model altogether. The plot does not sound very encouraging. It depends on young persons who wish to marry otherwise than their parents would suggest. This ancient theme Steele employs to exploit his campaign against forced marriages and duels. He confessed himself that he was mainly proud of a scene in which the hero rises above the desire to fight a duel. Judged in one way it is a priggish scene, and over-written, yet it must be remembered that Steele and his followers had a definite influence on restraining the practice of duelling. Morally the play is most commendable and it may be recalled that Parson Adams in Fielding's *Joseph Andrews* found that as a Christian he could commend it as 'containing some things solemn enough almost for a sermon'. Yet from the point of view of the theatre it misses the brilliance and glitter of the manners comedy of the Restoration. There were numerous other practitioners of sentimentality in the theatre. Mrs. Centlivre, for instance, gained success with a play entitled *The Gamester* in which the evils of gambling are displayed and the whole action is made dependent on the moral. The heroine promises to marry the hero if he will abandon the tables and ultimately shocks him into such action by dressing up as a man and so outwitting him that she wins from him her own picture.

More effective than the exaggerated moods of this sentimental play was the genuine domestic tragedy which constituted some of the most satisfactory dramatic production of the first fifty years of the eighteenth century. As has already appeared, this form of play had gained a certain vogue as early as the Elizabethan period but in the eighteenth century it developed a new realism in the hands of certain writers. These dramatists made a direct and genuine attempt, though most often with a melodramatic emphasis, to represent some aspect in the lives of the middle classes who were constituting an ever increasing part of the audience. One of the most successful of these writers was George Lillo (1693–1739), whose *The London Merchant; or The History of George Barnwell* (1731), had an apprentice as its hero. Lillo gained a European reputation with this play, and in England it was long popular in the theatre. Whatever its limitations and its crudity it seemed to open up the promise of new dramatic possibilities. Lillo followed it in 1736 with *Fatal Curiosity: A True Tragedy*, which is a stronger play. It deals with a rural couple who are overwhelmed with poverty. Their son who has been successful in the Indies returns to them in disguise and they kill him for his riches. When the error is revealed the husband kills his wife and then commits suicide. The play has many sentimental elements, as for instance a certain luxuriating in emotion. An outstanding example is the melodramatic incident of the son's return in disguise so that later he may have additional pleasure in revealing his true identity to his parents. At the same time one feels that here is a drama, honestly composed, with a stern tragic intention which triumphs over any excesses of expression and situation. Lillo answered some need not only in his own countrymen, for his influence spread to France and to Germany.

While the sentimental drama and domestic tragedy constitute the most original contribution in the first half of the eighteenth century other and more traditional types also had their place. The success of Nicholas Rowe has already been noticed. In *The Fair Penitent* (1703), and in his later plays he was looking back towards the tradition of tragedy of Otway, for whose work he expresses an admiration. The theme is derived from a play of Massinger's entitled *The Fatal Dowry*, and though it is a domestic theme, in the sense that it deals with a crisis in a number of private lives, it has a background that is romantic, and even heroic. The emphasis lies with the female character who dies for the sake of love and here emphasis is given to the pathos of her position. The play certainly had a great success in the theatre, though this may have been in part due to the acting of such brilliant players as Betterton and Mrs. Bracegirdle. Later in *The Tragedy of Jane Shore* (1713), which was 'written in imitation of Shakespeare's style,' Rowe gave to the domestic or private theme some gestures of an historical setting. The emphasis still lies on a woman and the pathos of her position. The same elements combine in *The Tragedy of Lady Jane Grey* (1715). Rowe had gifts as a poet and as a dramatist, but at times he seems uncertain as to whether he will restore older forms of drama or capitulate to the new tendencies which have developed in his age.

While Rowe attempted to compromise between two worlds others maintained firmly a classical tradition in tragedy. Ambrose Philips in 1712 produced with success *The Distressed Mother*, a play based on Racine, and this was followed in 1713 by Addison's *Cato*. The popularity of Addison's tragedy is now difficult to understand, for the verse is stiff, the theme has little dramatic vitality, and the characterisation is uninteresting. Yet the enthusiasm for this heavy classical tragedy was unbounded, and on its translation into Italian, German and French it met with considerable approbation on the continent. At home, political motives contributed to the success, for both parties wished to claim virtue and liberty as their own distinguishing qualities and apart from this the portrait of a philosopher had interest to the men of the Age of

Reason. Abroad the phenomenon of a regular classical play composed by an Englishman must have been a motive of curiosity that increased interest. But on the whole, while Shakespeare and the older dramatists remained popular, the production of new work in the tradition of high tragedy declined. Samuel Johnson in 1749 brought the blank verse tragedy of *Irene* with him to London as part of his literary assets, but despite the acting of his old pupil Garrick the play was not successful. Though much practised throughout the first half of the century the popularity of the heroic and classical tragedy was on the decline. Had some man of genius been associated with its history, its fortunes might have been otherwise, for the continued devotion of audiences to Shakespeare showed that there was a public for tragedy in the grand manner, when it had character and liveliness and a command of the theatrical art.

The contemporary attitude to the excesses of the diction of classical and heroic tragedy and the improbability of the situations can be seen in a number of parodies and burlesques. Of these the most effective was the burlesque tragedy of *Tom Thumb* (1730), by Henry Fielding, the author of *Tom Jones*. This entertaining piece, which was later reworked as *The Tragedy of Tragedies* or *The History of Tom Thumb the Great*, touched upon all the weaknesses in the more ambitious tragedy. Though in his own plays Fielding had little of the strength which marks his work in fiction he certainly possessed a genuine sympathy with the more sentimental and domestic types of drama. *Tom Thumb* had great popularity and encouraged Fielding to other burlesques.

Fielding was probably led to this type of entertainment

by the success of John Gay's ballad-opera *The Beggar's Opera* (1728). This is one of the outstanding achievements of the English stage in the early eighteenth century. Its immediate aim was to satirise Walpole in the person of Macheath, the highwayman. But it had a more subtle design in transferring the whole grandiose apparatus of opera to the precincts of Newgate. Gay may have begun the notion innocently and modestly enough from a chance suggestion given him by Swift, but he had fallen upon some new dramatic form which had great charm and on an idea which was effectively satirical, and in an unintentional way, half-revolutionary. *The Beggar's Opera* belonged not only to those things in the theatre which are original, but to that very small group of the plays which are permanent and have success whenever they are competently revived to intelligent audiences.

If the first half of the eighteenth century was weak in drama it could claim to have some outstanding figures among actors and actresses. The tradition in the early years of the century favoured excessive gesture, turgid declamation, and the extravagant exploitation of farce. This was modified by a few men of outstanding genius. A step in the right direction was taken by a remarkable figure, Charles Macklin, who if the records are to be trusted, lived to be over a hundred, and was engaged actively on the stage for over sixty years. He brought some degree of naturalness into the interpretation of Shakespearian parts. For instance, in the early years of the eighteenth century Shylock had been played as a comic part. While Macklin was not bold enough to destroy this tradition he had brought to it elements that were pathetic, so that one member of his audience wrote that 'the Jew's private calamities made some tender impressions'. David Garrick was the most memorable figure in the whole eighteenth-century theatre. This pupil of Samuel Johnson, who came with him to London, won his way with nothing except his histrionic talent to a place of national fame, a fortune and a funeral at Westminster Abbey. Of his power over audiences and of his great range and talent there can be no doubt. It might be urged that he subdued everything, author, play, and all to the actor. His career shows a notably varied range of performances of Elizabethan and other classical plays, but he performed them in his own versions. Great as were many of his interpretations of Shakespeare's characters it can be questioned whether he fully appreciated the greatness of Shakespeare's genius. He would have been a more faithful servant of the drama as a whole if he had been less ready to adapt the plays to his own liking, and if he had performed the plays in Stratford instead of setting in motion that strange masquerade of the 'Shakespeare Jubilee'. But Garrick is dead, and for the actor, unlike the author, the wonder passes as soon as he leaves the stage for the last time. It is easy for those who have not seen him to write critically, but had we been among the audiences of his time we should also have succumbed to the spell. He belongs to an age when the actor dominated the theatre, and that is not a healthy condition, for the theatre can only truly flourish when all the partners to the play work in unison.

The conditions in the later eighteenth century do not differ materially as far as the audiences and their taste is concerned from those in the earlier decades of the century. The prevalent demand was for sentimentalism and pathos, and these the dramatists supplied with outrageous extravagance. Such drama can contribute nothing to the permanent tradition of the national theatre, but it remains important only to the student of taste, while the student of the theatre may wish to be warned of the dangers and excesses which surround his art. Two of the most egregious practitioners were Hugh Kelly (1739–1777), whose *False Delicacy* (1768), had an enormous success, and Richard Cumberland (1732–1811), who was equally if not more popular in plays such as *The West Indian* (1771). In *False Delicacy*, Kelly presents a number of lovers who owing to their complications are maintained in a continuous emotional fret, from which neither they nor the audience are released. In *The West Indian*, a young man who delights in intrigue but is full of 'nice feelings' attempts to seduce a young lady. After a number of complexities the 'nice feelings' prevail, and he marries the lady only to discover by one of those chances, more common in the theatre than in life, that she is an heiress. With audiences satisfied with plays such as these there seemed no future for the theatre, or at least no future unless some man of genius appeared. Fortunately two such men of genius did appear, in Oliver Goldsmith and Richard Sheridan, and suddenly they make the seventies of the eighteenth century one of the distinguished periods in English drama.

All that criticism need say of Oliver Goldsmith (1728–74) is contained in the phrase in Samuel Johnson's epitaph: 'there was no type of writing that he did not attempt, and each type that he attempted he adorned'. With natural genius few men can have been so richly endowed, but the application and capacity for taking pains, which are necessary auxiliaries if genius is to be effective, were sadly lacking. In turn he produced essays, a novel, and poems in the heroic couplet, and into each genre he seemed to instil by some effortless means an original element which was the outcome of his own personality. In none of these forms did he persist. For instance, *The Vicar of Wakefield* is so fresh and human amid the fictions of the eighteenth century that one would imagine that the author would be impelled to go on and repeat his success. For him it was only a volume that, with the help of Johnson, he might sell to some rascally bookseller and so escape from debt, and he seems altogether unconscious of the fact that before the end of the next century over a hundred new editions of his masterpiece would be printed.

Goldsmith seems equally casual in his entry into drama. His own work is so full of genuine and recognisable emotions that one can easily understand that he had a deep antagonism to the false excesses of sentimentalism. When he came into the theatre with *The Good Natur'd Man* in 1768 it was with the deliberate intention of exposing the strained emotionalism of Kelly and Cumberland. Much in the play shows that Goldsmith is new to the stage and some of the scenes and motives seem not wholly to have detached themselves from the type of drama which he is out to attack. Still the satire was keen enough to be recognised by eighteenth-century audiences and they opposed a play in which their emotional indulgences were parodied.

Admirable in its period, *The Good Natur'd Man* has not the qualities to lift it into that small group of plays whose power of entertainment remains potent from one generation to another. It was otherwise with *She Stoops to Conquer, or The Mistakes of a Night* (1773) for this has given pleasure whenever it has been reproduced. It survives rough handling by the rawest of amateurs and yields a new vitality when the best of theatrical talent is devoted to it. The critics have found many faults in it, but then how easily the critics do discover these blemishes in great works of art. The most memorable thing that T. S. Eliot said about *Hamlet* was that it was imperfect, while A. C. Bradley once permitted himself the sentence that 'something of the confusion which bewilders the reader's mind in *King Lear* recurs in *Antony and Cleopatra*, the most faultily constructed of all the tragedies'. The task of criticism should be supremely to define the quality which has given certain dramatic works an abiding vitality. In *She Stoops to Conquer* this can be discovered first in the fable, which, whatever its improbability, is full of strong dramatic situations, easily intelligible, and all contributing towards a main design. This central story, endowed with an atmosphere at once natural and romantic, is full of that geniality and warmth which are continually such pleasing qualities in Goldsmith's work. The characterisation is strong and unmistakable, but within well-defined types an element of the original has been introduced. The whole combines to make a comedy, never pretentious, never over-subtle, but arising so solidly from what is fundamental in human nature that audiences in succeeding generations have always recognised its quality.

As has been emphasised more than once in this volume, there is very little English comedy that lives on from one generation to another. With the single exception of G. B. Shaw, those who have produced it, Congreve, Goldsmith, Sheridan, Wilde, all have had short careers. Of these one of the most brilliant is Richard Brinsley Sheridan (1751–1816), and his career is perhaps the strangest, as, unfortunately, it is one of the shortest. He was the son of an actor, and was sent to Harrow for his education. There, according to Lord Holland, 'he was slighted by the masters and tormented by the boys as a poor player's son'. As a result he had an aversion for the stage. If he refused to act in a theatre he became in real life involved in an adventure which has all the motives of an eighteenth-century comedy. To save the beautiful Elizabeth Linley from an undesirable suitor he eloped with her and went through a form of marriage. As a consequence he had to fight two duels to save his reputation, and later he fell in love with the lady whom he had been previously platonically protecting. In 1772 they settled in London, in the centre of the world of fashion, and sheer indigence forced Sheridan to turn to that world of the theatre which he had attempted to avoid.

His later career is less well-remembered. He abandoned the stage for politics, and became at one time or another Under Secretary for Foreign Affairs, Secretary to the Treasury, and Treasurer of the Navy. One could willingly have spared every one of those honours for ten years of comedy. As it is all that is important comes within four years: *The Rivals* (1775), *The School for Scandal* (1777) and *The Critic* (1779). To these can be added the short farce of *St. Patrick's Day* and the lively and successful comic opera *The Duenna*, both of which belong to 1775, the same year as *The Rivals*. In 1777, a few months before *The School for Scandal* was enacted for the first time, he prepared an adaptation of Vanbrugh's *The Relapse* under the title of *A Trip to Scarborough*.

Of *The Rivals,* which is a miracle as a first play, Sheridan's own opinion was very modestly expressed, and Moore in his *Diary* goes as far as to affirm that 'Sheridan always said *The Rivals* was one of the worst plays in the language and he would have given anything he had not to have written it'. It is a comedy which acts far better than it reads, and this accounts for the patronising tone of the opinion expressed by some contemporary periodicals. A typical example of this critical myopia appears in the *Gentleman's Magazine*: 'The dialogue of the comedy is, in general, natural and pleasing; as to the plot, though we have often heard of younger brothers and fortune-hunters assuming fictitious titles and estates as credentials to rich heiresses, it seems very unlikely that real rank and fortune should be deemed an objection, and therefore disclaimed as in the piece before us. Here the marvellous and the romantic seem to lose sight of the natural and probable.' The immediate popularity lay partly in the skill with which Sheridan combined the wit and elegance of a manners comedy, freed from all immodesty of the Restoration pattern, with scenes of sentimentality which could be played 'straight' or treated ironically. It is more difficult to account for the permanent power which the play has possessed over audiences in the theatre. Sheridan seemed to have some innate knowledge of the conventions of the stage. His characterisation is broad, and indeed in Mrs. Malaprop it may be urged that it is too broad. Still it consistently gives magnificent opportunities to the players. The plot, which would not serve for a novel, holds together admirably in the theatre. The exposition is quickly, even entertainingly, given and the purely comic plot is mingled with the sentimental.

The whole has elegance, and one is again reminded that while morals make men good, it is manners that make them interesting. One of the most original things in the play is the dialogue. This is Sheridan's own invention. It is sometimes said that Shaw makes all his characters witty or at least amusing, but so do Congreve and Sheridan and Wilde. If the characters talked as they would do in real life they would be unbearably dull, but a 'nice derangement of epithets' makes them entertaining and despite the fact that Sheridan is writing in prose he would seem to have learned from Shakespeare this way of giving a wash of fine words to the play.

As *Love for Love* is to *The Way of the World* so is *The Rivals* to *The School for Scandal*. The later play is more considered, more subtle, more perfect even, but less spontaneous. The farcical elements have been removed; the characterisation is firm, penetrating and human and, above all, the plot is one of the most perfect in the whole range of English comedy. Congreve, who had long considered the plot of *The Way of the World*, allowed his pattern to become so elaborate that elements of obscurity intruded, but Sheridan maintains a complex movement with complete clarity and shows the strength of his command particularly in episodes such as the famous screen scene. The characters, too, are penetrating portraits so that one must go back to Congreve, and sometimes beyond Congreve to Shakespeare, to find the like of Charles Surface and Lady Teazle. *The Critic* is a less ambitious play. It is a general burlesque on dramatic absurdities bringing up-to-date the parodies which in the previous century Buckingham had invented so successfully in *The Rehearsal*. Augustan tragedy, the sentimental drama, the incongruity of mismanaged stage effects, all these Sheridan burlesqued. It can still give entertainment as modern revivals have shown. There is no play which reveals more fully how Sheridan understood the stage and its conventions. English drama would have been far richer if he could have served it longer.

However uneven in dramatic creation, the late eighteenth century and the early nineteenth had some outstanding figures among their actors and actresses. Garrick was retiring by the time that Sheridan had captured the stage, but he wrote an admiring prologue to *The School for Scandal*. Edmund Kean was finding his way to the stage as a child player before the century had ended, and in the early nineteenth century gave commanding performances of the great Shakespearian roles, particularly Shylock, Richard III, Hamlet, Othello and Iago. Roger Kemble formed his own company as an actor and a manager in 1753, and through his marriage with Sarah Ward, became the father of one of the most distinguished of all English theatrical families. John Philip Kemble, his son, was an actor of the declamatory school, and played in all the major Shakespearian roles. He was overshadowed by his sister Mrs. Sarah Siddons, one of the great figures of the English stage. She had been engaged by Garrick in the seventies to play Portia at Drury Lane, and from then until 1812, when she gave a farewell performance in Lady Macbeth, she was a figure of incomparable power. Her friendship with all the great literary authors of the day, and the esteem in which she was held by the Royal Family did much to elevate the social status of the actor in the community, where unfortunately the theatre itself as an institution had but little standing. These were not healthy conditions, for as has already been suggested the theatre depends on a multiplicity of efforts all aimed at one end, and the lack of this cannot be compensated by the excellence of one contributor however brilliant that may be.

II

The Nineteenth Century

THE early nineteenth century is one of the most unrewarding periods in the English theatre. It was a great era in poetry and fiction, but men of letters when they came into the theatre seldom found themselves in a congenial atmosphere. The audiences were content with farce and melodrama and extravagant displays and no management had the courage to attempt any elevation in their taste. The legitimate theatres had been constantly enlarged so that natural acting was no longer possible, and spectacle and declamation could alone appeal to the large and sometimes unruly audiences that filled the vast auditoria of Covent Garden and Drury Lane. The players, apart from the brilliant exceptions, were too often a group isolated from ordinary society, and without adequate taste or education.

All the poets of the romantic period showed some interest in the theatre, but failed as dramatists. Shelley's *The Cenci* (1820) is the most notable of their achievements, both in drama and poetry, and if the incestuous theme had not been so forbidding the tragedy would probably have had a greater success on the stage. Coleridge and Wordsworth were far too self-centred and introspective to be successful in the theatre. On the other hand Byron, despite a formidable egocentricity, showed genuine knowledge of the stage and of its possibilities in plays such as *Manfred* (1817), *Marino Faliero* (1820), and *Cain* (1821). Keats delighted in the theatre, and had he lived he might well have matured his knowledge into a successful dramatic talent.

Part of their lack of success must rest with the romantic poets themselves and with their deliberate cult of individualism and an isolation from society. At the same time it must be admitted that the conditions in the theatre were invariably discouraging. Popular taste was attracted not by the best things in romanticism, but by gothic tales and horror themes and the ravings of the more lurid elements in German romantic tradition.

It is a commonplace that in the second half of the nineteenth century there was a renaissance of taste and of dramatic writing in the English theatre. All this can be admitted without unduly exaggerating the quality of the work through which the improvement was achieved. In order to maintain standards it is well to remember that in Norway Ibsen's *Catiline* was written as early as 1850, and *Pillars of Society* by 1877, and it is a sobering exercise to compare these with the best that was being written in England at the same dates. In England itself a number of new conditions contributed to improvement. By an Act of 1843 the restriction which had kept the approved performance of plays to the patent theatres was removed. Strangely enough the new liberty was not immediately realised, but in the sixties and in the seventies a number of new theatres were built. Unhappily it was not one of the choicest periods in English architecture, but whatever the structural deficiencies conditions were reached in which there was a freer trade in the presentation of plays. There was, further, an improvement in the quality of the audiences and the delight of the

Queen in dramatic entertainments tended to give the theatre a social standing which it had not possessed in the early years of the century. The position of the dramatist improved when from the sixties onwards he contrived to substitute a profit-sharing basis for a lump payment. The change made the profits of the dramatist comparable with those of the popular fiction writers, and had the system existed earlier in the century men such as Dickens and Thackeray might have been drawn to the theatre. Further, there existed, especially from the sixties, an increasing awareness of social problems, and some of this found expression in drama.

The earliest of the reformers who modified drama from the fustian of stale romantic themes, farce and extravaganza was T. W. Robertson (1829–71), who brought into his plays scenes which had a contemporary realism and gave them more modern methods of production on the stage. Something of this fresh quality was present in his earlier plays such as *David Garrick* (1864), and *Society* (1865). They gained fuller definition in *Caste* (1867), a play which when read seems to be full of gross exaggerations, but has a dramatic quality immediately apparent when it is revived on the stage. Robertson has given the play direction by adding to its comedy and sentiment a strong central theme based on social ideas. A working class girl, Esther Eccles, has married George D'Alroy who in rank is far her superior. The characters are grouped around these two personalities who represent social extremes. On D'Alroy's side is the haughty De St. Maur, and the reasonable Captain Hawtree. Among Esther's associates, apart from her inebriate father, there is her sister Polly with her solid working class lover Sam

ED-F

Gerridge. *Caste* is not a great play, but it is an enormous improvement on the theatre of its time, and it seems to set the drama on the task of social criticism in which during the next half-century some of its greatest triumphs were to be won. Robertson had achieved much both in theme and in the effective production of plays, yet it is sobering to remember that Ibsen's *Peer Gynt*, the greatest drama, perhaps, of the modern theatre, belongs to the same year as *Caste*.

Robertson was followed by Henry Arthur Jones, a playwright of good intentions and some melodramatic skill, for whom excessive claims have been made by the historians of the drama. In 1882, he produced *The Silver King* in collaboration with Herbert Herman. The play deals with a protagonist who falls on evil ways as a result of unhappy influences but makes good in America and returns to deal out retributive justice and revenge. Lest one should gain any exaggerated conception of the merits of this sentimental melodrama it is again well to remember that Ibsen's *An Enemy of the People* was produced in the same year. Jones's talent in the plays which followed is uneven, often pretentious and solemn, heavy and bombastic when he is serious, but with a talent for comedy when he is in his easier moods. In *Saints and Sinners* (1882), and in *Michael and his Lost Angel* (1896), he made his most serious attempts to deal with social and religious themes. Through Michael he shows a clergyman falling in love with a girl whom he has previously condemned. There is a fundamental unreality in the main conception despite theatrical effectiveness in individual scenes. This is true again of a play such as *Mrs. Dane's Defence* (1900), which has an admirably conducted cross-examination scene, though the theme as a whole never intrudes beyond melodrama into the theatre of the imagination. More effective is *The Liars* (1896), where he treats love and marriage and the conflict of emotions without the excessive self-seriousness of some of his other plays. It must be admitted that little either in his plays or in his personality remains attractive, but his contemporaries saw him as one to whom 'belongs a generous share of the credit for restoring the drama in England to its rightful position as a civilised and civilising art'.

A far more engaging figure was Sir Arthur Wing Pinero. He had a very long career which began in the late 'seventies and continued to *The Enchanted Cottage* of 1922. His wide range extended from farce in *Dandy Dick* (1887), to sentimentality in *Sweet Lavender* (1888). Stronger than these was *Trelawney of the 'Wells'* (1898) a play whose appeal has proved to have an enduring quality. Pinero in looking back in this play at the theatre of Tom Robertson, has allowed a warm and generous mood to instruct the action, and though sentimentality may be dominant, the whole has a genuine human quality which audiences have recognized whenever the play is revived. He had approached the more serious social and personal problems already in 1889 with *The Profligate*, but his greater success in this type of drama came later with *The Second Mrs. Tanqueray* (1893), and *The Notorious Mrs. Ebbsmith* (1895). By comparing *The Second Mrs. Tanqueray* with *The Profligate* one can discover what an English writer could learn on the technical side alone by the study of Ibsen. The whole management of a modern theme with a natural movement of the characters within a well-constructed plot has now come within the powers of an author who earlier had to rely on 'asides', and coincidences and innumerable entrances and exits. This increased skill in construction combines with a firm and sober treatment to make *The Second Mrs. Tanqueray* one of the best social or problem plays in the nineteenth century. Paula, the wife of Tanqueray, is a woman with a past, who is led ultimately to suicide, and though a modern audience may feel that the emotions are forced, they remain effective in the theatre, and Pinero, as usual, offers ample opportunities to the players.

While Henry Arthur Jones and Pinero were aiming at a play in which contemporary problems and conditions could be seriously explored, other traditions were also finding a new vitality of expression. William Schwenk Gilbert, who began his career as a writer of farces, developed an individual type of poetic and satiric comedy in *The Palace of Truth* (1870). The motive of the action lies in the phantasy that within the Palace of Truth each character must speak precisely what is in his mind. The play had a powerful dramatic influence. Gilbert employs it again, though not in such an obvious or direct way, in *Engaged* (1877), and it remains the dominant motive in a number of Shaw's early comedies such as *Arms and the Man*. Gilbert might well have developed into a considerable dramatist of a regular type had he not discovered a new medium for his talents. In 1875, he wrote *Trial By Jury*, and from then onwards he worked in collaboration with Arthur Sullivan on the 'Savoy' comic opera.. The wit and brilliance of these made contemporary dramatists realise that if they were to compete they must improve both in plot construction and in verbal dexterity. The English stage had not been so brilliantly entertained since Gay's *The Beggar's Opera*. The work of Gilbert and Sullivan has suffered from too frequent repetition, and there would be much to be said for the institution of some voluntary self-denying ordinance limiting the number of performances of the Savoy operas. Yet their very popularity is evidence of their appeal and of the fact that in English there is nothing that matches them.

Before the nineteenth century closed, one writer of comedy for a few years adorned the stage and then tragically disappeared. On the work of Oscar Wilde criticism still maintains considerable dispute, and yet whenever his comedies have been revived they have pleased audiences, even those whose minds were not held when they read the plays in the unrevealing pages of a book. Apart from his French play *Salome* (1892), his reputation depends on a small group of comedies: *Lady Windermere's Fan* (1892), *A Woman of No Importance* (1893), *An Ideal Husband* (1895), *The Importance of Being Earnest* (1895). Wilde's comedy is an intimate expression of his own personality. The plots may from some critical standards be deficient, and in the earlier plays he is occasionally beguiled into episodes which are sentimental, and even a little solemn. But from the first he is working out towards a comedy that shall be all compact of elegant artifice, and this ultimately he achieves in *The Importance of Being Earnest*. It was a return, not by any direct imitation, but by some innate sympathy, to the spirit of Congreve. But Wilde was hampered because his fashionable and well-bred audiences would not permit the dramatist to employ the amorous themes which Congreve pillaged as motives for entertainment. Wilde had to preserve a strait-laced decorum and yet achieve gaiety and wit. That he succeeded is a measure of the brilliance of his dialogue. Further he endowed comedy with a sense of good-natured amusement, of fun, of gay irresponsibility, so that his plays have not their like on the English stage. The dramatic critic may complain about construction and discover that Wilde still uses the antiquated device of the 'aside'. But in a comedy where all is artifice why should a complaint be lodged if in addition the dramatist uses the artifices of the stage itself? The solemn have shown with ponderous efficiency that Wilde had not the serious and moral aim which was developing in the social drama of his time. It would indeed have been inappropriate had he allowed these elements of the real world to intrude into this pattern of gaiety and entertainment. The test of drama lies ever in the theatre and any who will submit to that test with Wilde's comedies are likely to succumb. Those who mix up considerations about Wilde's life with his comedies are confusing two unrelated issues. As far as the drama is concerned, the tragedy of Wilde's life is that it removed him from the theatre when his contribution might have been so much more ample and varied.

12

G. B. Shaw

THE greatest figure in English drama in the late nineteenth and in the twentieth century is unquestionably George Bernard Shaw. His is the longest career in the British theatre, for his first play *Widower's Houses* was begun as early as 1885 and his most recent work *In Good King Charles's Golden Days* appeared in 1939 over half a century later. Throughout the whole of the intervening period he was engaged in dramatic production, and apart from his work as a creative artist he made contributions of outstanding importance as a critic. *The Quintessence of Ibsenism* (1891, revised 1913) had an important effect on the development of Ibsen's reputation in England, while Shaw's weekly articles in the *Saturday Review* from 1895 to May 1898, collected in 1931 as *Our Theatres in the Nineties*, are at once the most brilliant and most painstaking series of notices ever composed by a regular critic of the contemporary drama.

His earliest work in drama was directed towards the statement and criticism of contemporary social evils: in *Widower's Houses* he dealt with slum landlordism; in *Mrs. Warren's Profession* (1894) with prostitution, and in *Arms and the Man* (1894) with the romantic conception of the soldier. Amid these early plays *The Philanderer*, in which the misconceptions of Ibsenism are mingled with a certain egocentric display, is of more ephemeral interest. In the other plays, after an uneasy start in

Widower's Houses, he proved to himself, though not immediately to the public, that he was a dramatist of great power and originality. From Ibsen he had learned how to manage the stage for plays with a contemporary setting, and scenes which admit discussion as well as action. From his predecessors in England there was little that he could learn except to discover that with Wilde he shared a brilliance in dialogue. Unlike Wilde he was determined to use this verbal gaiety not merely for entertainment but to explore every known problem, social, moral, political and religious. He had an ear for all the rhythms of speech, and his friendship with Henry Sweet, the philologist and phonetician, led him to study the ways in which dialogue could be made as natural in movement as it was witty in content.

In character, he seemed at first to work a little more to a formula. He studied the conventional conception of a character as it appeared on the stage and in the minds of the public, and then inverted it for the purposes of his own challenge to the lethargy in contemporary thought. For the romantic courtesan he substituted the hard-headed business woman, Mrs. Warren, and for the guardsman of Ouida, who emerged from action with his uniform in parade-ground perfection, he showed the conscript who knows hunger, fear, dirt and despair. It was as if all his characters were passing through Gilbert's 'Palace of Truth' and disclosing themselves unashamedly as they were. The satiric effect of his characterisation was undoubted, even if it was obtained at some loss of human depth and variety. A warmer and fuller conception of character was obtained in *Candida* (1890), a play in which he subjected himself more deeply than before to

Ibsen's influence. It was through the production of *Candida* in New York in 1903 that Shaw began to capture the theatre, and the American success led Granville Barker to introduce the play into a series of matinées at the Royal Court Theatre.

In the next phase of his development Shaw departed from the contemporary scene to portray historical figures though maintaining the same formula of inversion as he had first employed in *Mrs. Warren's Profession*. The nineties had almost worshipped a romantic conception of Napoleon, and so in *The Man of Destiny* (1895) Shaw presented a satiric portrait of the young Bonaparte which mocks at the grandeurs and idealisations. In *The Devil's Disciple* (1897) he showed how melodrama could be converted into a play through which thought and discussion could be conveyed, and then in *Caesar and Cleopatra* (1898) he made his most considerable attempt up to this period in the presentation of an historical character. His mind had turned toward Shakespeare's writing down of Caesar in *Julius Caesar* and to his magnificent and romantic portrayal of the mature Cleopatra in *Antony and Cleopatra*. Shaw contrives, with a fuller plot than he usually employs, to give a conception of Caesar which is impressive and yet full at the same time of comedy.

Already, as the portrait of Caesar showed, his mind was moving towards philosophical problems. He had worked out for himself a dynamic conception of evolution in which man's will need not be idle in the settling of his destiny. If man would be but alert and active, the life force would use him in the unsteady and uncertain fight towards Progress. Still indulging in an atmosphere of luxuriant comedy he explores these ideas in *Man and*

Superman (1901–3), one of the most brilliant of all his plays and unclouded by the deeper vision which appeared after the war of 1914–18. The play was a success in both England and America, and Shaw, on publishing the play, seemed to give proof that his genius was inexhaustible by adding a third act 'Don Juan in Hell', and an 'Epistle Dedicatory', with a 'Revolutionist's Handbook', and 'Maxims for Revolutionists'. The philosophical life-force theme gained a briefer, but dramatically an effective, presentation in *The Shewing-Up of Blanco Posnet* (1909), and here a touch of sentimentality, very rare in the plays, gives a human quality to the action.

Shaw's other plays before 1914 gave evidence of great versatility. Already in *You Never Can Tell* (1896) he had shown that his comic genius could have an almost irresponsible exuberance. In the later plays the exuberance remains even when a social theme is elaborately explored. So in 1906 there is gaiety in *The Doctor's Dilemma* where the Shavian attack on the medical profession is presented, and again in *Misalliance* (1910), which has education as its theme. In 1912 *Androcles and the Lion*, with its massive preface on Christianity, gives at times an entertainment which is farcical without ever abandoning its main purpose of exploring the nature of religious faith. Some urged in these years that the plays were merely brilliant speeches. This was altogether to miss the skill with which discussion had been made dramatically possible by a great command of the stage. Nowhere is this more clearly shown than in *Getting Married* (1908), where action, as ordinarily understood, is reduced to a minimum, while the dialogue and interplay of the minds of the characters maintain the interest of the audience.

Three plays of this period showed a more solid narrative basis in plot. *John Bull's Other Island* (1904) was Shaw's dramatic exploration of the Irish problem. *Major Barbara* (1905), looking back towards the methods of 'inversion' in character portrayal, showed the ways of a millionare munition manufacturer and his Salvation Army daughter and of their several contributions to society. Of more permanent interest, in that its theme was detached from social and political problems and rested in the human personality as such, was *Pygmalion* (1912). This play may have begun with the jest that phonetics are a clue to class distinction, but it seizes with whatever Shavian transmutations on the old fairy-story theme of the poor girl who became a princess.

During the war years 1914–18 it would seem that Shaw did not write a new play. He came back to the stage with *Heartbreak House* (1918), a satiric comedy in which he had used his study of Chekhov's *The Cherry Orchard* to give his impression of the futility of peoples and policies in post-war Europe. Though audiences in England failed to detect it, there was an increased depth of vision in the play which resulted from all that Shaw had felt and contemplated during the war years. In 1921 with *Back to Methusaleh* he produced his most elaborate dramatic creation, in which he goes back to the very beginning of things and forward as far as thought can reach in order to show the nature of the life force and its effect on the destiny of man. Shaw in his preface reviews his past achievement in drama and regards this series of plays as its culmination. He confesses that he had intended *Man and Superman* to be a dramatic parable of Creative Evolution, but 'being then at the height of my invention and comedic talent, I decorated it too brilliantly and lavishly'. Now he abandons Don Juan for the Garden of Eden and, in a more tragic period of human history, offers man a new myth without the erotic associations of the previous theme. The play was produced in all the main centres of theatrical activity in the world, and it aroused such interest that its appearance marks the height of Shaw's reputation as a dramatist. The series of five plays which constitute the work cannot be easily performed in the theatre in a run of less than three evenings, and it is a tribute to Shaw's genius and reputation that managements and public have on several occasions combined to revive the cycle. As frequently he moves from comedy to a movement of rhetoric which has in it an element that is solemn and almost sublime. So here in the concluding speech of Lilith: 'Of Life only is there no end; and though of its starry mansions many are empty and many still unbuilt and though its vast domain is as yet unbearably desert, my seed shall one day fill it and master its matter to its uttermost confines. And for what may be beyond, the eyesight of Lilith is too short. It is enough that there *is* a beyond.'

In 1923 *St. Joan* was produced, and this was perhaps the most popular of all Shaw's plays. In the person of the 'Maid' he had constructed a character which served all the purposes of his thought, and yet remained an attractive and credible human person. The complex historical actions with which she was concerned he had simplified into six superbly clear dramatic scenes, and only in his 'epilogue' did he revert to his normal practice of the presentation of ideas through comedy supreme over characterisation. He allowed a quality warmer and more romantic than is usual in his work to suffuse this play. The last group of plays, *The Apple Cart* (1924), *Too True To Be Good* (1932), *The Millionairess* (1936, and *Geneva* (1938), have an increase in discussion, though an experienced dramatic skill maintains the dialogue within a pattern acceptable to the theatre.

To his own generation he has been a great figure and he has given more delight in the theatre to the world at large than any man of his time. His limitations are obvious. He does not touch tragedy, possibly because he has a certain physical fastidiousness, which amounts almost to a fear of any world which cannot be uncontrolled by his own thought. The brilliance of his dialogue sometimes leads him beyond the bounds of dramatic propriety so that the stage becomes a hustings. He has kept romance and colour out of his plays deliberately, and so failed to give the visual artists of the theatre, the designers and costume-makers the opportunities of collaboration which they would have delighted to possess. It is churlish to insist too sternly on this side of the balance sheet for one who has given so much delight and to whom every man of his generation is to some degree indebted. The merits of his achievement can fortunately be studied continually in the revivals of his work, and it would seem that many of his plays will enter into the permanent repertory of the English theatre.

13

English Drama in the Twentieth Century

OF THE English theatre in the twentieth century this at least can be said, that it is better than the English theatre in the nineteenth century. The art of the theatre still works uneasily inside the entertainment industry. It suffers from the inroads of speculators and of commercialism, and especially in the provinces it has carried on an uneven competition with the films. There are many towns of a considerable size in England to-day without a professional theatre of any sort, and children often 'complete' their education without seeing a play acted by living and professional actors on a stage. Yet the art of the theatre has developed especially during these last two decades. Methods of production have improved, and the composition of original plays of merit has been considerable.

The theatre has indeed survived despite the conditions which have been imposed on it. The prices to which speculation forced up the rentals of theatres in the West End of London during the twenties and the thirties made the production of classical or experimental plays a difficult and dangerous venture. But fortunately the theatre did not depend solely on the West End of London. At Birmingham, Liverpool, Manchester, there were Repertory Theatres in which work of originality and distinction could be produced, while outside the fashionable centre of the West End, Miss Lilian Baylis developed at the Old Vic, and later at Sadler's Wells, an organisation for Shakespeare and the classical drama, as well as for opera and the ballet. Further, the public in London showed that it was prepared to go out as far as the Lyric Theatre at Hammersmith when such a delight as the revival of *The Beggar's Opera* was prepared for its entertainment.

At the same time it would be false to portray a picture of unrelieved gloom at the centre of London saved only by interesting work on the periphery or in the provinces. Some writers of serious problem plays such as John Galsworthy contrived to compete with the other attractions offered by the commercial theatre, while in comedy Sir James Barrie and Somerset Maugham, the one with sentiment, and the other with a cynicism that sometimes delved into satire, made themselves popular dramatists and yet contributed to the art of the theatre. Further, there have been bold experiments in the whole art of play production beginning with the season in April 1904 of J. E. Vedrenne and H. Granville Barker at the Court Theatre. It was during that season that G. B. Shaw gained an opportunity of reaching larger audiences in the theatre, and later he was to find his place as a successful competitor for a place in regular West End productions. The adventures which Granville Barker began were followed in later years by others who loved the art of the theatre and were determined, despite financial conditions, to see that it prospered.

An outstanding example can be found in Sir Barry Jackson's raid on the London theatre from Birmingham in 1921, including a production of Shaw's *Heartbreak House*. Whatever may have been the financial results the adventure was artistically successful. It is well to remember that this was achieved in the period after the war of 1914–18 when the theatre had been booming, and when speculative rentals made sober and enduring management almost impossible. It was on 29th December, 1920, that *Chu Chin Chow*, which had survived the war, created a record in being produced for two thousand performances, and in the same year another spectacle, *The Garden of Allah*, based on Robert Hichens' novel, proved so popular at Drury Lane that the traditional 'Lane' pantomime had, against all precedent, to be taken to Covent Garden. The devotion of actors and dramatists to their own art was evidenced by the formation of numerous societies for the Sunday performance of plays for which it had been found difficult to find a hearing at the regular theatre. Granville Barker had commenced such Sunday performances through the Stage Society as early as 1898, and some of these Sunday productions proved sufficiently impressive to tempt the managers to offer regular 'runs'. There were frequent examples of the inability of the commercial managers to assess popular taste, and one of the most successful plays of the whole period, R. C. Sherriff's *Journey's End*, was turned down by almost every commercial management in England, before it proved one of the great successes of the whole period.

In the field of dramatic composition the outstanding figure was G. B. Shaw, whose work has been already considered. Among other writers one can distinguish a group which continued the tradition begun by Robertson, Jones and Pinero of dealing seriously in the theatre with contemporary social problems. Harley Granville Barker, whose work extended over the whole range of the theatre, as actor, producer and critic, had completed *The Marrying of Ann Leete* as early as 1902. In this comedy a young girl of an upper middle class family rejects her official suitor for a match with her father's gardener. A certain air of fancy which surrounds this play is missing from the grim outlines of *The Voysey Inheritance* (1905), which deals with a young lawyer who discovers that his father has been misapplying the funds entrusted to him by his clients. He determines to continue the policy in order to save his father's reputation. William Archer saw the merit of this play on its first production and commented: 'A great play, conceived and composed with original mastery, and presenting on its spacious canvas a greater wealth of observation, character and essential drama than is to be found in any other play of our time'. *Waste* (1907) in which an illegal operation causes the death of the mistress of Henry Trebell, a brilliant young politician, proved too strong a theme for the censor. The play itself, which ends with Trebell's suicide, has an atmosphere of unrelieved gloom. *The Madras House,* which followed in 1909, proved the most successful of all Granville Barker's plays. Complex in theme, bold and original in treatment, it may be best described as a satire on the thwarted lives led by women in England in the first decade of the century. Granville Barker's theatre may not be completely satisfying, but it is so original that one could wish that he had persisted. In his 'Prefaces' he became one of the great Shakespearian critics of his time, but this was little compensation for the lost dramatist, and however gloomy some of the plays may be, there are other elements, such as his collaboration with

Laurence Housman in *Prunella*, which show that he had a romantic side to his nature.

John Galsworthy came to the theatre with *The Silver Box* in 1906 after he had gained a considerable reputation as a novelist. For a quarter of a century he produced well-contrived dramas on current social questions and the London managements accepting his plays found them reasonably successful with their audiences. Since his death Galsworthy's reputation has suffered a remarkable eclipse. It is true that in his lifetime excessive claims were made for his achievements, and further, in any objective and critical reckoning he will be found far more effective as a novelist than as a dramatist. Still, the plays reached a steady level of technical competence. Unlike Aristotle he believed that character and ideas were more important than plot, and so as a result most of his plays depend on a rather obvious and even mechanical design. From this character emerges, never in independence and variety, but rather in a set 'humours' form, in the Jonsonian sense of the word, as if each person had to answer one step in an argument. The central theme deals invariably with some fundamental problem of social justice, but the exploration often allows sentiment to become dominant over intellect; such were *Strife* (1909), *Justice* (1910), *The Skin Game* (1920), *Loyalties* (1922), *Escape* (1926), and a number of other plays.

Galsworthy served an immediate purpose in awakening audiences to the urgency of the questions which were poised in his plays. Yet he remained solidly fixed in the world-which he criticised and its ultimate values he accepted. The drama was held in tightly by materialism, and by that limited conception of realism which dealt solely with a contemporary scene, usually in a middle-class setting. This tradition of bourgeois realism was a strong one, and is to be found in a number of other writers. St. John Hankin in plays such as *The Return of the Prodigal* (1905) shows himself the successful satirist of the middle classes. Stanley Houghton, a dramatist discovered by Miss Horniman's Gaiety Theatre at Manchester, gave effective expression to the revolt of youth against the dinginess of its provincial and middle-class setting in *Hindle Wakes* (1912). St. John Ervine contrived to elevate this drama of criticism into a grim prose tragedy in *Jane Clegg* (1913) and *John Ferguson* (1915).

On the whole it was to the period before the war of 1914–18 that this drama of middle-class realism properly belonged. It was continued into the twenties, but by then more imaginative minds were aware, as was shown in *Heartbreak House*, that there were other problems more spiritual and more fundamental to the existence of civilisation also to be explored. Thus though Galsworthy continues to the end of the twenties, and St. John Ervine produces *The Ship* in 1922, and while an interest attaches to a newcomer such as C. K. Munro, who in *At Mrs. Beam's* (1921), gives a comic portrayal of a London boarding-house, the main original impulse of this type of drama has been supplanted by other forms. Already as early as 1908 in *The Tragedy of Nan*, John Masefield had given an imaginative, even poetic quality to a drama of rustic realism. There is a certain incongruity between the grim, domestic setting and the prose medium on the one hand, and the rhythms and imagery of the language which seem to look back to the ways of the Elizabethan playwrights. Masefield's tragedy was an implied protest against the realism of the 'Manchester' school and all those who regarded the stage solely as a means of exploring middle-class problems.

There was one figure who, after some initial failures, had long maintained an almost effortless conquest of the London stage, and had never admitted that the theatre could be held within the confines of realism. Sir James Barrie had produced *The Professor's Love Story* as early as 1894, and his success had been continuous for nearly thirty years to *Mary Rose* in 1920 and *Shall we Join the Ladies?* in 1922. Only later with *The Boy David* did he seem to lose contact with the audiences of his time. In the decades of Barrie's success he had produced a great variety of drama. With *Peter Pan* (1904), he had invented a new child's mythology, while in *Mary Rose* he had combined fantasy with a comment on the future life which had made a wide appeal to audiences who had lost friends and relations in the war. In *The Admirable Crichton* (1902) he had dealt with the problem of social castes and individual worth, but in a more whimsical way than Tom Robertson had employed half a century earlier. He had a very cunning mastery of the modern stage and of the effects which it could produce, as he showed in *Shall We Join The Ladies?* This skill he used to create a world of his own where sentiment dominated as in *Quality Street* (1902), though often it could be found blended with irony as in *What Every Woman Knows* (1908). He is probably seen at his best when the one restrains the other as in *Dear Brutus* (1917). To see the plays now is to feel that they belong to a lost world, of kindlier and more gentle emotions, but the theatrical skill that controlled them is still apparent.

The element of poetry and fantasy present in Masefield and Barrie gained a far stronger expression in the group of Irish dramatists whose work from the beginning of the century was associated with the Abbey Theatre in Dublin. The whole movement has been admirably described in Miss Ellis Fermor's *The Irish Dramatic Movement*. The most imaginative minds of the group were W. B. Yeats, J. M. Synge and Lady Gregory, though their work did not penetrate to the centre of the English theatre. Yeats's supreme poetical genius moved uneasily in the theatre, but his enthusiasm for the movement was unbounded. He was determined to break away from the realism by which so much English drama seemed caught into a new world. As Miss Ellis Fermor has written of him, 'the Irish drama had not only a founder, and an acute business man and a courageous fighter, but, something without which these would have been barren, a visionary poet'. In his own plays Yeats probably remained mainly a lyrical poet even in the theatre, and audiences are likely to enjoy *The Land of Heart's Desire* (1894), *The Countess Cathleen* (1899), *The Shadowy Waters* (1906), and the later plays more for the beauty of the verse than for dramatic situations. In J. M. Synge poetic imagination combined with great dramatic power. One of Yeats's great services to the Irish drama was to discover Synge in Paris and send him to the Aran Islands where somewhere he discovered that strange imaginative language which gives beauty to his plays. He had a genius for comedy and tragedy: the one appears in *The Shadow of the Glen* (1903), and *The Playboy of the Western World* (1907), and the other in *Riders to the Sea* (1904), and *Deirdre of the Sorrows* (1910). It may be unwise to attempt to distinguish between the merit of two gifts so original and valuable as the comedy and tragedy of Synge, but it may without ingratitude be confessed that the comedy wears better. The tragedy seems a little self-conscious, even sought after, but the comedy has a virile and permanent quality and remains as impressive and original as when it was first conceived.

While Synge's contribution was outstanding the Irish theatre produced other playwrights of merit. Lennox Robinson, the author of a number of plays, captured the London' stage with his comedy *The White-Headed Boy* in 1916. Lord Dunsany, while he relied on a less directly Irish inspiration, still maintained, in plays such as *A Night at the Inn* (1916), a world removed from the stubborn realism which held captive much in English drama. Further, Lady Gregory herself, while her main inspiration lay in the encouragement of others, was herself a writer of plays.

Apart from the Irish theatre the more poetical drama, both in prose and verse, has had only a fitful and uncertain existence in England in the twentieth century. Stephen Phillips, a poet of unstable temperament and of too facile a talent, had succeeded in the early years of the century in re-introducing blank verse drama to the London stage. Sir Herbert Beerbohm Tree performed his *Herod* in 1900, and the torrent of praise from both the critics and the public is now difficult to grasp. There followed in 1902 a production of *Paolo and Francesca*, which, written as early as 1898, is possibly the most successful of Phillips's dramas. Then in rapid succession came *Ulysses* in 1902, *The Sin of David* (1904), *Nero* (1906), *Faust* (1908), and *Pietro of Siena* (1910). Phillips, who had been himself an actor in Sir Frank Benson's company, understood the possibilities of the modern stage and exploited them fully, and his verse had a large-sounding rhetorical quality. He might well have developed had not his own intemperate habits driven him to work in an irregular and forced manner. His fall from popular esteem has probably led to an excessive severity in recent judgments on his work. John Drinkwater also worked in poetic drama. The success of his *Abraham Lincoln* in 1919 depended in part on the appropriateness of its theme in the post-war period. Neither *Oliver Cromwell* which followed in 1922 nor *Robert E. Lee* in 1923 had a similar success.

A new recruit from Ireland arrived in the twenties in the person of Sean O'Casey. Though he employed prose as his medium it was prose with an unmistakeable poetical quality. *Juno and the Paycock* and *The Shadow of a Gunman* in 1925 were followed by *The Plough and the Stars* in 1926 and a number of other plays which included *The Silver Tassie* of 1928 and *Red Roses For Me* (1946). His plays had a strange mixture of realism with romance and symbolism, and of prose with imagery and poetic imagination. He seemed to re-live the urban life of Dublin, and yet at moments bathe it in a light that belonged to Shakespearian drama. Similarly he could indulge in comedy, even farce, and yet hold the audience with profound sentiment that ranged from the ironic to tragedy. He had a great command of the stage, and over language he exercised a compelling power, so that the cascades of bright words seemed to overflow from his plays.

Among the more recent English practitioners of poetic

drama an outstanding contribution was made by T. S. Eliot in *Murder in the Cathedral* (1935), which was followed by *The Family Reunion* in 1938. Eliot abandoned the blank verse of the romantics and rediscovered for drama a language full of natural rhythms and a vocabulary close to that of ordinary idiom. His invention in plot and character were not equal to the ingenuity and appropriateness of his diction. *Murder in the Cathedral* had considerable success with a small, selected audience, but *The Family Reunion* in which classical mythology is mingled with a modern setting fails to be fully convincing. Among younger writers W. H. Auden made a number of experiments in bringing verse back to the stage. He employed, as did Eliot, all the rhythms of the colloquial language and to these he added movements discovered in popular songs and dance tunes. His most successful experiment was *The Ascent of F*6 (1936), which he wrote with Christopher Isherwood. The conception is incomplete but the play has a number of comments on the problems of a troubled decade and the whole seems to be feeling its way to some new expression in drama.

While the poets experimented not without success it was other playwrights who gained the main commendation of the popular stages. Somerset Maugham had established himself in 1919 with *Caesar's Wife* and *Home and Beauty*. These were comedies of an elegant life in which cynicism mingled with commentary. They were followed by two accomplished comedies in which the idle rich were effectively exposed. Of these *The Circle* (1921) is one of the most finished plays which Maugham ever wrote, while *Our Betters* in 1923 shows how heartless and degenerate is the world in which his cunningly contrived comedy so skilfully moves. At times he seems to have returned to the moods of Restoration comedy, though one feels that he lacks gaiety, and that he despises these puppets who provide the wit which he contorts with a genial malice. He made an easy capture of the commercial managements and his success lived on from the 'twenties to the 'thirties.

Somerset Maugham had to compete in the twenties with a newcomer, Noel Coward, who in many ways is the most accomplished man of the theatre in the period between the wars. He, above all others of his generation, understands the whole instrument of the modern stage, and he has shown himself equally accomplished in his mastery of films. *The Vortex* (1923), first gave him a reputation as actor and author and showed that he could write with study of character and concern for a problem. But mainly in the twenties he applied himself to such light-hearted comedies as *Fallen Angels* (1925), and *Easy Virtue* (1926). When, after the economic catastrophe of 1929, the mind of the country became more serious, Coward responded with *Cavalcade* (1931). It may be urged that his quality of mind and his sensibility are not equal to his great theatrical skill, but it must be conceded that Noel Coward has probably given pleasure in the theatre to a larger number of people than any other man of his generation.

Among the new dramatists of the thirties were two promising but contrasted figures, 'James Bridie' (O. H. Mavor) and J. B. Priestley. 'James Bridie' in *The Anatomist* (1931) had shown a great power of evoking emotion in a play based on the careers of Burke and Hare. This he followed by a large number of plays in which comment and fantasy mingle with excellent dialogue and comedy. In *Tobias and the Angel* (1931), and in *Jonah and the Whale* (1932) he shows how individual was his approach, and how humour and poignancy could combine. The same strong originality marked *Mr. Bolfry* (1943), a play which delighted audiences in the war years. Here he seems to transfer the Faustus story to a modern Scottish setting, adding his own humour and whimsicality. J. B. Priestley entered the London stage in the same year as 'James Bridie'. He followed a dramatic version of his popular novel *The Good Companions* (1931) with a quick succession of plays, some of the most notable of which are, *Dangerous Corner* (1932), *Laburnum Grove* (1933), *Eden End* (1934), *I Have Been Here Before* (1937), *Time and the Conways* (1937), *Johnson over Jordan* (1939), *They Came To A City* (1943) and *An Inspector Calls* (1946). These are only a selection from Priestley's dramatic output. While some thought that he had come only accidentally into the theatre he showed that he intended to stay, and that he could produce prolifically. Basically his main aim seems to be to explore human character, particularly in relation to the structure of society. Yet he is not another Galsworthy, for he possesses a half-concealed poetic quality which comes through in symbolism in such plays as *Johnson over Jordan* or *They Came To a City*. Further he is occupied metaphysically with the concept of time, as can be seen in a play such as *Time and the Conways*. Indeed, this element is never far from his mind, and sometimes it seems strangely lodged in his solid Yorkshire temperament which delights in a broad characterisation and a solid comic dialogue such as Dickens might have enjoyed. Priestley has a high standard of dramatic skill, but somehow one is always expecting that he will do better than he has previously done. It is as if some 'fatal facility' prevented him from reaching to greatness.

Somewhere this chronicle must end. These last years are too close to enter into a narrative which attempts briefly to summarise the achievement of centuries. This can at least be asserted: the State, at long last, has come in to help the drama to establish itself. The Customs authorities no longer levy the Entertainments Tax from companies organised on a non-profit-making basis whose work covers a general and rather vague formula of 'educational and partly educational' production. Further, the Customs authorities have made a valiant effort to interpret their own regulations humanely. Yet the whole incidence of the Entertainments Tax remains a subject of much controversy.

Nor has government aid ended there. For during the war, State funds were found through C.E.M.A. (Council for the Encouragement of Music and the Arts) to assist the wider distribution and the improvement of standards in Music, Drama, and the Visual Arts. In 1946 C.E.M.A. was incorporated under Royal Charter as a permanent body, entitled The Arts Council of Great Britain. From its funds assistance can be given to genuine non-profit-making companies which wish to enact the best of the past or encourage what is original and adventurous in the new. There are signs that an enlarged audience for the theatre is developing. England still remains insufficiently provided with theatres, and with schools of acting and design, but there are stirrings. From them there may yet develop, on some adequate scale, that co-operation of audience, actor, technician, producer and author from which a drama that adequately affects the national life may emerge. I conclude this study in a year when Covent Garden is established as a Charitable Trust, when the 'Old Vic' and the National Theatre Committee have joined in active co-operation, when the London County Council has granted a site for the National Theatre on the South Bank of the River.